Hum

D0559937

OPERA PSYCHOTHERAPY

OPERA PSYCHOTHERAPY

BARTALINI

Illustrated by the Author

Exposition Press   *Smithtown, New York*

First Edition

© 1981 by Gualtiero Bartalini

All rights reserved. No part of this book may be reproduced, in whole or in part, in any form or by any means, electronic or mechanical, including photocopying, recording, or by any information storage and retrieval system, without permission in writing from the publisher. Address inquiries to Exposition Press, Inc., 325 Kings Highway, Smithtown, NY 11787.

Library of Congress Catalog Card Number: 80-70716

ISBN 0-682-49703-7

Printed in the United States of America

In Order of Appearance

OPERA PSYCHOTHERAPY

Prelude

If you've read Havelock Ellis, Adler, and Freud,
Jung, Watson, and Pavlov, and head-shrinking boys,
You'll begin feeling guilty, sinful, and lewd,
Culpable, criminal, steeped in foul turpitude.

In flagrante delicto, an old Latin phrase,
Means caught with your pants down, a mere paraphrase.
We all have committed a crime of some kind,
If not in reality, at least in our mind.

This guilt, culpability, fear to have sinned
Gets a stranglehold subtly; gets under the skin.
So instead of consulting a head-shrinking dope,
Start going to opera; don't abandon all hope.

Music hath charm to soothe savage breasts.
It dispels fears and terrors and phobias' unrest.
It's a cure to be sure, this I do guarantee.
It brings surcease and peace and tranquillity.

You'll see murderous rakes; masses burned at the stake;
Jealousy, madness, abductions, heartaches;
Inquisition and torture, lust, suicides;
Guillotined nobles and demented brides.

Sleepwalkers abound. One, engaged to be wed,
Walks her way, fast asleep, into a stranger's bed.
Potions and poisons flow fast and free
With a love and death motive for two hulks at sea.

You'll witness beheadings, smotherings, raids,
Girls going insane, stabbings, grim ambuscades.
This is all set to music, the greatest that's known.
What more can one ask for, for one's soul to atone?

You'll save yourself lying on couches, I vouch,
Listening to hogwash by some head-shrinking slouch.
You won't have to drool, or spout silly things
To some "Herr Professor" or your town dingaling.

Your soul will be soothed, your morals as well.
All the horrors you'll see will be mere bagatelles.
You'll see corpulent Mimis expire with TB.
You'll laugh yourself well, just take it from me.

La Traviata

Madamigella Va-le-ry
Gave all for love, but not for free.
She did things that she hadn't ought,
This dear, expensive, French cocotte.

Her name is Violet Valery,
But not a shrinking violet she.
Her brow ain't wet with honest sweat;
She charges guys for what they get.

In the first act—that's based on fact—
Violetta's at a party.
She's light and gay, so *negligé,*
So debonair—so tarty.

She drinks to sin—adulterin'
At the party she's at
With gents that lust—the upper crust—
And *femmes hors de combat.*

She meets a guy who's young and shy,
Who starts to woo the lady.
She falls in love, this turtledove,
Whose past was oh, so shady.

She's overwrought—this gay cocotte—and
Sings, "Love is so much hooey."
But just the same, the dame is game.
Perhaps, *"E forse lui?"*

How can she tell—this demoiselle—
If it's the real McCoy?
After she's stepped—been kept and slept—
With cash-and-carry boys.

She's more than fond, this courtesan,
Of life and fun and sin.
"It's folly to be wise," she sings,
Then leaves it ALL—for him.

But it's too late. The three wise fates
Have put their heads together
And what they've brewed and steamed and stewed,
No Violet could weather.

Someone, it seems, has spilled the beans
To stuffy Germont *père*.
He starts right out—the grumpy lout—
To catch them in their lair!

So on the scene—peevish and mean—
Seeks out the Jezebel.
But little did he think he'd find
So cultured a gazelle.

He meets the doll—the femme fatale—
Whose past was oh, so shady.
But he's astound' at what he's found.
Like Edie, she's a lady.

The martinet starts the duet
About his daughter pure and fair;
An angel straight from paradise,
About to get the boot—the air.

The groom's a slob—also a snob.
He'll jilt the bride-to-be.

" 'Cause Al's affair," he fumes and swears,
"Would ruin him socially."

We hear her say, "No, no, *jamais*.
Please go away. I've done no wrong.
Besides, I'm ill. I'm taking pills.
The doctor says it won't be long!"

Mid tears and cries he pleads and sighs;
Assures Vi love is fleeting.
Time wounds all heels—yields lousy deals.
"What then?" he keeps repeating.

Is he surprised—can't believe his eyes—
To read she's sold her property;
To have a home that's not a House and
Live in respectability.

He's heard that tarts have noble hearts
And even more—a soul.
Besides the other things they've got,
They all have hearts of gold.

He proves his point. She'll blow the joint.
She'll pay the piper's price.
We hear her say, "The woman pays."
She'll make the sacrifice!

The father mean is now serene,
Grateful he's made the deal;
"Have a nice day; you'll be okay,"
Then marches on—the heel.

With choking throat Vi writes a note,
"Dear Alfred, please forget.
I thought I loved you, but I don't.
That's how it is, my pet."

As Alfred reads, he starts to seethe.
He's furious and sore.
He'll make her pay. She'll rue the day,
That double-dealing ————!

Deep in despair, he pulls his hair.
His dad again appears,
"Come to my arms, my beamish boy.
Let's get away from here."

It's now Act Three, and now we see
Violetta at a ball.
Although she flits, she's torn to bits.
She fears there'll be a brawl.

She's with Douphol and that took gall—
An ex-amour—and now
A baronet—bound to protect
The tarnished Violet somehow.

Al, too, is there, hides his despair,
But plans to make a scene.
"Come one and all," tipsy, he calls,
And here he vents his spleen.

"See you this dame? Know you her name?"
"Indeed we do, V I O L E T T A."
"Well, after all we did and done,
Behold she's paid—vendetta."

Then, indiscreet, throws at her feet
The loot he's won at cards.
"Oh, what a gall," cries out Douphol.
"I'll settle this canard!"

Then Violet swoons to Verdian tunes
That melt a heart of stone.

6

While all her friends gather and bend,
Alfredo mopes alone.

This is the cue: pistols for two,
Or swords, if he likes best.
"We'll meet at dawn, you Satan's spawn."
Douphol says, "Be my guest."

Here once again old dad drops in.
How did the prude get there?
To see the ladies of the House
At Flora's pied-à-terre?

It sounds absurd, but still you've heard
How father's sins visit the kids.
But this may be a double take.
The father visits them instead.

At any rate, dad made a date
And just in time to scourge his son.
"No gent should treat a dame that way,
You popinjay, you jerk, you bum."

"What have I done?" He's overcome.
Alfredo's filled with shame, despair.
Too late he learns she loves him still.
He's torn to bits. He leaves with *père*.

It's now Act Four. Vi's at death's door.
She knows the end is near.
"Good-bye," she sighs, for days gone by,
Also to her career.

Her doctor friend tries hope to lend.
He tells her she'll get better.
But it's too late. Those hags, the fates,
Are on their way to get 'er.

From 'twixt her breast a note she wrests.
She's read it o'er and o'er.
"Forgive our trespasses," it says.
It's from the prude—the genitor.

"You've kept your word, Alfred has heard.
The duel took place at dawn.
Take care. Sit tight. You'll be all right.
We're on our way. *Bon chance*. GERMONT."

"Too late," she cries and wipes her eyes.
"*Addio*. Good-bye. Farewell.
Oh, happy days. Oh, sultry nights.
Good-bye, my clientele.

"Oh, joy supreme," we hear her scream,
"Alfredo!" In he flies.
It won't be long. Soon she'll be strong.
All wrongs he'll rectify.

Oh, joy. Oh, glee. They'll leave Paree.
Her health he'll soon restore.
She starts to cough. The trip is off.
She sinks unto the floor.

Before she dies, mid sad good-byes,
She gives her love her effigy,
That he may think of her sometime
While playing with some chickadee.

She's never out of breath, it seems,
Tubercular though she may be;
Sings forte and pianissimos
And often gets right up to B.

"In heaven above," she tells her love,
While bitter tears are flowing,

"I'll pray for you." She has no doubt
That's where —nonstop—she's going.

It won't be long. It's her last song.
They'll meet again, but how and when?
Al knows his dove will fly above
Like the repentant Magdalen.

Faust

ACT I

Faust's Study

This is the house of the lecherous louse,
The venerable, hoary philosopher Faust.
He's surrounded with skulls, test tubes, and vats,
Ancient parchments, chemicals, dead rats, and bats.

For years upon years he's tried, and he's sick,
To try to discover what makes humans tick.
He's consulted the stars; dissected the dead.
The answer is *"Warum,"* and is his face red!

He gets good and sore, so he curses some more;
Curses man, time, and science—over and o'er;
Curses love, curses space, and the whole goddamn race.
Der Herr Doktor Faust is a Freudian case.

He trembles and quakes, has arthritis and aches,
Has insomnia and spends his nights wide awake.
"So to hell with it all," he sneers in dismay.
"I've had it," he moans. "So I'll call it a day!"

"I'll mix my own poison and swallow it quick."
But there's many a slip 'twixt the cup and the lips.
He mixes the drink; then he wavers and shrinks.
He hears girlish voices and that makes him think.

11

The disgruntled old alchemist, cold misanthropist,
Regrets things of the world and the fleshpots he's missed.
So he calls to the devil to come to his aid.
He'll sell his old soul for youth and a maid.

The devil, who's always alive and alert,
Arrives on the scene, lively and pert.
"Me voici," says the devil—in this case he's French.
"At your service, *docteur. Voulez-vous* a young wench?

"Are you afraid of me, hoary *docteur?*
I look like the devil, I know, but, monsieur,
I'm at your service, so don't hesitate.
I can give you a deal, if you'll cooperate.

"I came when you called, *mon maître,* so speak."
"I'm a skeptic," says Faust, in a tenory squeak.
"I've no need of riches, glory, or fame.
However, you may be of use just the same."

"Très bien," says Mephisto. "What would you have, then?"
"A chicken," says Faust, "not an old boiling hen.
I crave young caresses, to tell you the truth;
Something tender and lively in bed. I want youth!"

So right then and there, without moving a hair,
A vision of beauty appears in the air.
It's "Gretchen am Spinnrad," the sweet Marguerite,
Turning the wheel with her two dainty feet.

The ancient Lothario falls nearly apart.
The vision's too much for his ancient old heart.
"It's a deal," he tells Satan. "Now what do I do?
The sooner the better. It's all up to you.

"How *gemütlich,"* says Faust, the lascivious swine.
"She's right up my alley. *Zo wunderschön—Hein?"*

"Take it easy," says Satan. "Sign your name on that line;
Right on those dots, just below Proserpine's.

"Don't forget what I say; you've the devil to pay;
Of course, not on earth, you old boulevardier.
I'll be within sight, both day and at night,
But down there where I live, your soul's mine—all right?"

He hands Faust a scroll, impish and bold.
Der Herr Doktor signs and forfeits his soul.
Faust then drinks a brew from the devil's own hand.
At once he's turned into a dashing young man.

With that simple dose, Faust is metamorphosed
Into a youth—handsome, charming, jocose.
He says, "When do we start this *gemütliche Fahrt?*"
"Right now," says Satan. "Get ready to start.

"Have your last fling," we hear Satan say.
"You asked for it, so let's be on our way.
You'll have love and romance—dance in a swirl—
In this the best of all possible worlds."

ACT II

The Kermesse

Not even the Breughels could paint such a scene
Of drinking and dancing, with laughter and screams.
There are burghers and students; soldiers and Fraus;
The whole scene's alive; *sehr freundlich;* a WOW!

Amid all this revel appears Valentine,
Marguerite's brother, grave, dull, saturnine.
He's there among soldiers, students, Siebel.
He's going off to war and he's surly as hell.

13

He's as gay as a crutch, like a man who's in Dutch.
He holds a medallion (not going to help much) .
It's a gift from his sister, the chaste Marguerite.
It's supposed to protect him. (We'll see how *tout de suite*.)

His one greatest worry is leaving the town
Where his ancestors died, but he can't stick around.
Deutschland über alles. But he begs of his friends,
"Keep an eye on my sister." (She'll need more;
   you'll see when!)

Siebel is a boy; wears collar and tie;
Sings lyric soprano. (Some folks wonder why.)
He loves Marguerite, picks dainty bouquets.
Siebel, I dare say, has got to be gay.

Mephisto appears, full of charm and good cheer;
Distinguished, *soigné*—a real cavalier.
His aim is to please, and he's always at ease.
With devil-may-care, he starts shooting the breeze.

Derisive and bold, full of hell, he begins
To sing of the calf of gold, of all things.
He sings how the monster stands up and derides
The whole human race and even the skies.

He laughs as he sings of the bold golden calf;
How the human race grovels, goes crazy, and daft;
How they snivel and kneel—debased human heels—
While the devil conducts, as the veal laughs and squeals.

With cynical charm he starts reading palms;
Predicts death and destruction, fears and alarm.
To Siebel he says, "Every flower you touch
Will wither and fade at your very first clutch."

With arrogant stride, he scoffs and derides.
To that jerk Valentine, he's ruthless and snide;

Predicts he'll be killed by someone he's met;
Tells him where he can stick Marguerite's amulet.

He then strikes at a cask that starts pouring wine.
He sneers as the revelers all get in line.
They jump and they bump; it's a real turnverein.
Everyone's merry, except Valentine.

When Lucifer mentions the name Marguerite,
Valentine jumps from his seat to his feet.
"Enough is too much," shrieks the grumpy *soldat*.
"I'll settle his hash right here on the spot."

The imp with his sword makes a ring on the ground.
They start fencing and dancing, around and around.
Valentine's sword is smashed right in two.
He's madder 'n hell; the chorus is, too.

Everyone's gauche, but not at a loss.
The men turn their swords, forming a cross.
The devil is cowed, as you may well expect.
He cringes away. That did it, by heck!

With ants in the pants, stirred up in advance,
The overhauled Faust can't wait for romance.
"Take it easy," says Satan. "She's coming this way.
Remember, don't rush, just do as I say."

The sweet Marguerite is walking alone;
Modest and shy, she's on her way home.
Her eyes are cast down like the maiden forlorn
That once milked the cow with the two crumpled horns.

The lustful old boy can hardly stand still.
He rushes the Fräulein without cunning or skill.
Says he, "Fair demoiselle, may I escort you home?"
"*Nein,*" replies Marguerite. "I can manage alone."

"You blew it," said Satan. "Though she's not very bright,
Your impatient advance set her afright.
Marguerite, I have found, is not very profound,
But she can tell a pass from a hole in the ground."

ACT III

The Garden Scene

The first on the scene is the "boy" friend, Siebel,
Stripping Marguerite's garden of flowers, pell-mell.
He makes a bouquet, between *tour jetés;*
Then finds they are withered and dead—in dismay.

"That devil," he says, "lived up to his tricks,
But I'll fool him yet." So both hands he dips
In a basin of water that's blessed, on the wall.
The flowers revive, alive, and that's all.

Marguerite's boy soprano leaves the bouquet
On Marguerite's doorknob, then flounces away.
Faust and the devil appear on the scene,
With evil intent, as by now you've foreseen.

"Please leave me," says Faust to Mephistopheles.
"Without you somehow I feel more at ease."
The salacious, remodeled Herr Doktor Faust
Sings a heart-melting song to the dear humble house.

How chaste and demure, innocent, pure;
"Salut, demeure!" sings the old troubadour.
It touches his heart; he's truly impressed;
It's just like the little gray home in the West.

Though he'd like to renege, the devil says, "No.
The die has been cast, and that's how it goes.
Besides, I have brought a case of rare gems;
Just wait till she sees them. You're in, young old man."

16

The fair Marguerite again enters the scene.
"I wonder," she sighs, "who that guy could have been.
Perhaps he's a knight. And what might be his name?"
She picks up the spindle, reflects, and declaims.

She then sings a song of a king in Thulé;
A futzy old guy but faithful, they say.
His dear sweetheart died, and so he had made
A cup of pure gold, engraved and inlaid.

When he drank from the cup, as everyone knows,
He wept and he wept till the cup overflowed.
He died of old age, and as Death hovered near,
He took the last sip and died, the old dear.

Marguerite then gets up after spinning away
And finds on the door the garden bouquet.
"How sweet of Siebel to pick them for me,"
Then suddenly says, "What's this that I see?

"A casket of jewels. From whom can they be?
Rhinestones, how brightly they shine," murmurs she.
"I dare not look in, but I'm dying to see."
How could she know it was diablerie?

She tries one by one—jewels can be fun;
A girl's best friend, too, but Maggie's so dumb.
"I wish that somehow that guy saw me now.
He'd think me a princess. I know it somehow."

Frau Martha comes in, is startled and grins,
"Who gave you those jewels, Gretchen, *mein Kind?*"
"I must put them back, Frau Schwerlein," says she.
"They've been left by mistake; they can't be for me."

Frau Martha Schwerlein, as you later will see,
Was hardly a safe *dame de compagnie.*

17

She was chosen as guide by that drip Valentine;
'Bout as good as a hole in the head, Frau Schwerlein.

Mephisto tells Faust as they come through the gate
That that addlebrained Martha he'll use for a bait.
"*Gnädige* Frau, are you Martha Schwerlein?"
She replies that that's she; he goes on with his line.

"The news that I bring you, my dear charming Frau,
Is not very cheerful, that you will allow.
Your much beloved husband, dear lady, is dead,
But sent you his greetings." "That *Dummkopf*," she said.

"What else did he send me?" said Martha Schwerlein.
"Nothing," says Satan. "That's truly unkind.
You must find a replacement, dear Frau, yes indeed."
"I couldn't agree more," said she flippantly.

Meanwhile Mephisto throws Faust the first cue;
With devilish tact tells the guy what to do.
"Take her arm, you dumb cluck" (he means Marguerite's) .
"The battle is won. Get going, *tout de suite*."

At first Marguerite acts shy and discreet;
As the hotpot approaches, she tries to retreat.
"Please don't go away," he begs her. "Please stay.
Do you live here alone?" he asks. "Please do say."

She tells him her brother has gone off to war,
Her mother is dead, then goes on some more.
How she lost little sister—an angel was she.
It's all very touching—also touching is he.

He touches her arm; she escapes in alarm.
Then he tells her he loves her, with finesse and charm.
He sounds so convincing, and she is so dumb,
She believes every word. The worst is to come!

Mephisto is mad as the devil can be,
"She was right in the sack, and you let her flee."
But all is not lost. Marguerite reappears.
She opens her window and dreams without fear.

When Maggie's in doubt, she consults marguerites;
Plucks petal by petal so dainty and sweet.
She believes in the message those petals express;
Hers never say no; they always say yes!

"He loves me," she sighs, as she looks toward the sky.
Then all of a sudden she spots Faust and sighs.
She opens the door, only a notch;
Faust enters, but not for a mere kaffeeklatsch.

You can rock-a-bye-baby on the treetop,
But without a consort, the whole thing's a flop;
And though millions believe the Holy Ghost tale,
Only one that we know of got by with it—"Hail"!

ACT IV

Pregnant, abandoned, she's left in the lurch.
She's shunned by the faithful as they enter the church.
To make it still worse, she hears demons call,
"Marguerite, you are jilted," they say, one and all.

The soldiers return, triumphant, in line.
Among them is surly and dull Valentine.
The first one he sees is the faithful Siebel.
"Where is my sister?" he asks. "Please, do tell."

"Perhaps she's in church," answers Siebel.
She stumbles for words—how can she tell?
"That's just like Marguerite," then says Valentine.
"For my safe return she's praying. How fine.

19

"Let's trot along home, my good friend," says he.
"But why do you look so woeful at me?
Why do you falter? Speak. What is wrong?
Why must I not enter my house? Come along!"

But murder will out and sometimes the truth.
Val learns the worst, as the bard says, "Forsooth!"
He has no compassion—that clod, that galoot.
Siebel pleads and begs him have pity, en route.

"Who done it?" he cries. "I'll murder the guy.
He'll pay through the nose. For this he must die."
Mephisto and Faust are back on the scene.
With devil-may-care, Mephistopheles sings.

With sardonic leers, he laughs and he sneers—
A strange serenade that Valentine hears.
The song has a sting, and he ruthlessly sings,
"Before you give kisses, be sure there's a ring!"

And just like the devil, he doesn't relent.
He heaps insult on injury with evil intent.
"It was fun while it lasted," he sings. "Do you hear?
Now you must pay the piper, and pipers come dear."

"What do you here?" bursts forth Valentine.
"Your song's for my sister. Take this, you swine."
Mephisto's guitar he smashes in two,
Then, pointing to Faust, says, "Now I'll settle you."

The medallion that Marguerite gave him one day,
He pulls from his neck and casts it away.
Then, pointing to Faust, says, *"Und Du, schweiner Hund!"*
Both draw swords, and Valentine falls moribund.

The neighbors rush out. Val's drawing a crowd.
With his very last breath he keeps crying out loud

Maledictions, damnations at poor Marguerite,
Who loses her mind and goes nutty *tout de suite.*

ACT V

Marguerite's thrown in jail for infanticide.
In a vision she sees her rejuvenized
Faust, the seducer, the stranger unknown,
Who gallantly offered to escort her home.

The devil—the fiend—and *der Doktor* as well
Have entered, invisible, Marguerite's cell.
In a state of confusion, she's as nutty as can be,
So both Faust and Mephisto urge her to flee.

"The demon," she cries, as her mind she regains.
"I've had it," she screams, wants no *auf Wiedersehen.*
She drops to her knees; to heaven she pleads.
Her cries reach the skies; the saints intervene.

Not only the saints but Herr Goethe does, too.
He sends her to heaven. What more can he do?
The dirty old man will burn for his lot,
And this is the end of a hell of a plot.

Madame Butterfly

ACT I

Do come with me across the sea
To dear old Nagasaki.
Meet Cio-Cio-San, pride of Japan,
And drink her health with saki.

From the U.S.A. one fine day
Arrived the U.S. Navy;
With it, a Yank with stripes and rank.
He rikee misbehavey.

He meet'em man with fix'em plan
To marry Japan rady.
Yank say okay; he give'em pay.
Broker bow deep. He shady!

Consul he try to emphasize
Put something hot on ice.
Roll in the hay, he say, okay,
But later not so nice.

Who's telling who just what to do?
My country 'tis of thee.
America forever.
Drink health to bride and me.

With quaint allure, shy and demure;
With parasol and fan,

She makes her way across the bay,
Enchanting Cio-Cio-San.

"Oh, happy day," everyone say.
"*Bonzai* to Yankee man."
Bend very low. Walk on tiptoe.
Play tune on samisen.

All drinking tea, raw fish from sea,
Tempura, sukiyaki.
Very polite; some getting tight;
Too many drink hot saki.

But what is this—this noise, this hiss?
Across the bridge he comes;
Screaming a curse, abuse, and worse,
The fuming Uncle Bonze.

"You faithress one. What have you done?"
He points to Cio-Cio-San.
"You cast'em smirch on Shinto church.
You marry 'Merican."

The Bonze—the beast—the Shinto priest,
Rolling from side to side,
"*Ka misaronda sico, so.*
You phony, cockeyed bride."

"Get out, get out," the Yank cries out,
"You prancing marionette.
Karate you, that's what I'll do.
I'll teach you etiquette."

Then one by one, sulky and glum,
The guests follow the priest.
They scorn and shun poor Butterfly
And leave the wedding feast.

24

Rutenant say, "All go away."
He very nice; he Yankee.
He carry Cio-Cio-San inside;
Then both make hanky-panky.

Then one fine day, he go away
But promise come back soon,
When robin redbreast making nest
And cherry brossom broom.

ACT II

Three years go by, and Butterfly,
She wait and wait and wait.
Three times red robin making nest,
But Pinkerton, he late.

Then by and by another guy.
Rich man name Yamadori,
He rikee marry Butterfly;
Got yen. He hunky-dory.

Then consul guy come back and try
To reading bridegroom note
Terring about a Yankee bride
Coming with him on boat.

With great fatigue he starts to read.
She stumps him from the start.
He just can't make her realize
She's jilted, so departs.

Her faithful maid comes to her aid.
"You marry Yamadori.
He ugly so, but he got dough."
But Cio-Cio-San ignoring.

Suzuki say, another day,
"You marry rich man maybe?"
"Oh, no, me Missi Pinkerton.
Me marry. Me have baby."

Poor Butterfly, she start to cry.
Suzuki crying, too.
"Don't cry," say Madame Butterfly.
"Groom come. I promise you."

Suzuki sigh 'cause she know why,
So asking Missi, "How you know?"
"I know," say Madame Butterfly,
" 'Cause fortune cookie tell me so."

Then by and by, Suzuki, sly,
She say, "Can be Rutenant fake?
I not say fortune cookie lie,
But sometime cookie make mistake."

"The moon and I," say Butterfly,
"Knowing he come back soon. You see.
If not come back, maybe me die
Rike papa—make hara-kiri.

"Me not tell joke. Soon you see smoke
Coming from boat from sea."
Then Butterfly say, "Listen why,"
And start to singing *"Un bel di."*

"Why you not preese sing Japanese.
What for Itarian song?
You sing high note, maybe break throat.
Beside," Suzuki say, "too rong."

Then pretty soon, hearing big boom,
Big boat arrive in port.

"You see?" say Madame Butterfly.
Suzuki only making snort.

So here and there and everywhere
Brossom and cherry broom—
Across the floor, in front of door—
To welcome Yankee groom.

Then all night long, waiting till dawn,
Making big hole in screen;
Looking with hope, with telescope,
For husband from Marine.

At break of day, Suzuki say,
"You up all night; preese go take rest.
I call you when he come," she say,
Then make kabuki face, depressed.

Alas, alack, he did come back.
But not alone—the heel.
His blushing bride is by his side;
Her name is Kate—so shy, genteel.

"Three years ago I told you so,"
The consul looks askance.
"You sang, 'My country 'tis of thee.'
Who's sorry now, hot pants?"

"Ah, woe is me. What do I see?
My heart is torn with pain."
Too touched to face poor Butterfly,
He sneaks away again.

Butterfly soon, rushing in room,
Thinking he's come—her mate.
He came all right but got uptight,
So he passed the buck to Kate.

"Who is this dame? Preese, why you came?
What for you in my house?"
She learns the worse—the Shinto curse.
The lady is his spouse!

To make things worse and more perverse
Kate hangs around awhile;
Then blithely asks poor Butterfly
If they might take the child.

And Butterfly—she does not cry—
Just say, "Come back for baby soon."
She knows alas that all is past;
The Shinto curse has sealed her doom.

Yes, Butterfly say she must die,
So she make hara-kiri.
Everyone cry; not one seat dry;
All people feeling teary.

Curtain come down. No one make sound.
Then Butterfly come back;
Making big bow; throwing kiss, kowtow.
Everyone crap, crap, crap, and crap.

Tosca

Giuseppe Giacosa and Illica, too,
With Signor Puccini and also Sardou
Got into a huddle and cooked up a stew
Mixing fiction with fact. *Chacun à son gout.*

But why quarrel with trifles—if true or untrue,
The plot is a corker—a hullabaloo.
There's love, lust, and passion, and some torture, too;
Political snares; and a false *pas partou.*

There's blood and there's thunder and catastrophe.
The opera tears passions to tatters, you'll see;
Intrigue and deception and skulduggery;
Read on, gentle reader, this hot potpourri.

ACT I

The lover's a painter in love with a dame
Named Floria Tosca, a diva of fame.
He sings, as he paints, of strange harmonies,
But tenors are strange; I'm sure you'll agree.

The villain's a baron, a chief of police,
And he's hot for La Tosca, the great cantatrice.
His passion's for real; it's not a caprice.
And his project is worse than the rape of Lucrèce.

The runaway convict is l'Angelotti,
A political prisoner—a *corroboree*.
He escapes to a church and runs vis-à-vis
To the painter, the liberal, Cavaradossi.

"Remember you me and our camaraderie?
We fought side by side," sighs l'Angelotti.
"Has prison and pain made such changes in me?"
"Ye gods," Mario cries. "Of course. Now I see!"

They shake hands and vow with warm bonhomie.
He'll come to the aid of the party, says he!
A box lunch he hands him and tells him to flee.
"Quick, hide in the niche of the Attavanti!"

"The chapel is ours," he replies without brag.
"My sister has left there a fan and a bag
With women's apparel; disguise for a hag.
She said to wear them and run, if you have to in drag."

A voice is now heard. The timing's absurd.
It's Tosca, the diva, the jealous songbird.
She enters distraught, distracted, disturbed;
Calls Mario a two-timing, terrible word.

"I heard voices and fluttering skirts sneak away."
"Oh, come now," says Mario. "Please don't be that way.
I adore you. How could I my siren betray?"
They embrace and in parting we hear Tosca say,

"*Ciao*, my beloved, my sweet Sybarite.
Tonight in my villa, we'll make it a night.
We'll bill and we'll coo as two lovebirds might.
Come to the stage door to fetch me, all right?"

He then calls the jailbird, "Come out; it's okay.
My jealous enchantress is out of the way."

30

Then right at this moment they halt in dismay.
A cannon is fired. Cops are on their way.

"The manhunt is on. You must get away.
Go jump in the well," we hear Mario say.
"The well's in my garden. I'll show you the way."
Both hop, skip, and jump along the pathway.

In church, by the way, the Te Deum turns gay.
The frolicsome faithful put on a ballet.
"Such antics in church," we hear Scarpia say.
"Such sacrilege, heathens. Cut out that horseplay!"

He bursts in the church like a bat out of hell.
He'll slay, draw and quarter, the red infidel.
He knows where he's at; he's followed the smell.
In no time at all, he'll be back in his cell.

She's back on the scene; Miss Tosca, I mean;
Runs smash into Scarpia, the bigot supreme.
He drools at the mouth, mean and obscene.
What luck. A decoy. A go-in-between.

"Oh, Tosca divine. Let your hand touch mine.
I offer you water blessed from the shrine."
With these words the tyrant maps his design;
Nefarious, subtle, evil, malign.

He holds in his hand a beautiful fan
Which he found, he tells Tosca, on Mario's stand.
Her burning suspicions he fans with the fan.
Two birds with one stone he'll kill if he can.

He goes on to say that her lover did play;
Had a roll in the hay with a blonde yesterday.
Her rage knows no bounds; swears he'll rue the day;
Then runs from the church as the fuzz kneels to pray.

31

ACT II

Scarpia's having a bite by dim candlelight
In his palace abode, feeling mean and contrite.
How could he foresee his plan for delight
Would be his last supper, his very last night?

By his *salle à manger* he has what one might say
A homey idea of an *auto de fé*.
His houseguest is Mario, arrested today.
He screams in B flats while they torture away.

She's back on the scene, Miss Tosca, his dream.
'Twas Scarpia's idea, the lecherous fiend.
He'll coax and he'll scream till she spills the beans
Then have for himself (you know what I mean).

He knows all about the old lays of Rome,
But he plans to add one more lay of his own.
But prayers and appeals melt not hearts of stone.
Bereft and alone, she cries and she moans.

The superb *Vissi d'art* she starts tearing apart.
Lying prone on the floor with tears and Del Sarte,
She wiggles and tries to melt his hard heart.
He couldn't care less; so one asks, "What is art?"

Her cries of despair reach the skies, rend the air.
She recalls all the good deeds she's done here and there.
It's indeed odd of God, she sings in despair,
To be left all alone in the lurch; it's unfair.

As the pig continues the cruel third degree,
There's a shrill scream of pain. It's C above B.
It's the voice of her lover, Cavaradossi.
She's had it, then sobs, "In the well," helplessly.

The torture is o'er. Then bleeding and sore
Her lover limps in, dripping over with gore.
She runs to his aid and confesses once more
That she spilled the beans to the inquisitor.

"Dear God, what you've done, my cherished loved one.
You've betrayed us and lost the battle hard won."
"Enough," cries the fuzz, the copper, the scum.
"To the gallows the painter. Let justice be done!"

"Now, Tosca," says he, "it's between you and me."
"What's the price for his life?" in a daze murmurs she.
"The price for his life is as simple can be.
It's you, my proud beauty; I hope you'll agree."

Distraught and distracted beyond all degree
She pleads with the pig to let Mario free.
"Upon that condition," he chortles with glee.
She knows she's defeated; she nods, meaning *si*.

Delighted, the lecher, the mean debauchee,
Writes the safe conduct, the planned mockery.
He goes to the dame with the false assignee,
Breathes heavy, and sighs, "Now sock it to me!"

In the meantime our Tosca distraught as can be
Picked from the table a knife secretly.
So 'twas she and not he that stuck it in, see?
Take that, you old monster. You son of a B.

She's settled the score, as he sinks to the floor
Dead as a door nail, the lecherous bore.
"So you made all Rome tremble," she snorts and she roars.
"*Requescat* in peace, on your posterior."

She looks down in dread to make sure that he's dead.
She then places two candles alight by his head,

Snatches the pass from his right hand outspread,
Then cautiously leaves in a slow-measured tread.

ACT III

Getting ready to die as the dawn breaks the sky,
Mario sings as he cries of his nearing demise.
Life never was sweeter, he moans, and he sighs
For voluptuous Tosca, the light of his eyes.

He sings of the stars so bright in the sky.
He's truly upset. Who can figure why?
All through the song he gripes and he cries.
For some unknown reason, the guy hates to die.

While shedding hot tears a voice now he hears.
It's Floria Tosca, her steps drawing near.
She falls in his arms, starts wiping his tears.
With love and caresses, she calms all his fears.

"Do banish your fears and sad thoughts, dearest pet."
Then she whispers, "I killed the vile martinet.
The thing that he asked for he sure didn't get,
But I got the pass, love, with blood, tears, and sweat.

"We're as free as the air," she sighs in his ear.
"Here is the pass. The coast is all clear.
Together we'll cross this lousy frontier.
Now listen to me, my brave musketeer.

"The shooting, my love, is only a sham."
Surprised, he says, "Really? Well, gee. I'll be damned."
"It's all in the bag, adored one, my lamb.
When they shoot you, drop, then later we'll scram.

34

"When they shoot you, fall down; that's what I mean.
Don't move; lie still, just like a sardine.
When the soldiers have gone, I'll rush to the scene.
Then together we'll fly to safety, unseen."

The soldiers march in, take aim, and then stand.
They're given the signal; they fire at the man.
He falls to the ground; the action is grand.
They march away proudly, according to plan.

Fearful and breathless La Tosca appears.
"You've played your part well. Don't move yet, my dear.
They're now out of sight. The coast is all clear.
Get up, my beloved, arise. Don't you hear?

"My God," Tosca screams. "They've shot him for real.
The vile double-dealers, the villains, the heels."
She screams and she cries; she yells and she squeals.
Her oaths reach the skies; her own doom is sealed.

The murder is out. She's done it and goofed.
The thugs point to Tosca, defiant, aloof.
"No more will Cock Robin connive, threat, and spoof,"
She snarls at the henchmen, then jumps off the roof.

EPILOGUE

And now that you've followed this opus all through
I'd like if I may say one thing or two.
The characters are, I confess, all too true.
They lived, loved, and died as all mortals do.

The bloodshed, the intrigue, the agony, too,
Are a lot of malarkey—contrived ballyhoo.
Not one of those mentioned did what's what to who.
That's nothing but Sardou doodley-do.

Samson and Delilah

ACT I

The city of Gaza's the opening scene.
The Hebrews are threatened, defied, and demeaned.
They're affronted and menaced by the vile Philistines.
A fight to the finish is predicted, foreseen.

Even then they were struggling it out to obtain
The strip of the Gaza again and again.
Their one hope was Samson, the heavyweight swain,
Who developed his brawn but neglected his brain.

The Hebrews were beating their breasts at the Wall;
Their cries and laments filled the air like a squall!
They depended on Samson, who hated to brawl,
Saying, "Trust in the Lord. He'll settle it all!"

The Philistines feared the heavyweight jerk
With the strength of a bull (a most secretive quirk).
The Hebrews at last got mad, frantic, and irked
As the heavyweight champ flexed his muscles and smirked.

The Satrap of Gaza made the Jews sore as hell.
"God couldn't care less," said the hostile rebel.
In the chaos that followed, the battle to quell,
Samson slayed Abimelech, the snide infidel.

He then hastened away. A victor was he;
So he went off to slay his tribe's enemies.

The high priest of Dagon cried, "Curses on thee!"
To Samson, the hero of the Is-ra-el-is.

The Philistines gathered and worked out a scheme:
"Cherchez la femme!" said one of the team.
"Who else but Delilah, the harlot supreme?"
"Of course, let's get going!" cried the smart Philistines.

Delilah, the wanton, was ready to go.
When a man asked a favor, she'd never say no.
Yes, indeed, she knew Samson. In fact, time ago
She was jilted by him, just in case you don't know.

The Philistine meanies were bound and hell-bent
To discover the secret of Samson's great strength.
It was up to Delilah to brainwash the gent.
"This is grist to my mill," she said as they went.

By hook and by crook word reached Samson's ear;
He was told that Delilah still loved him most dear,
That she never forgot his muscles and hair.
The flattery did it; he'd rush to her lair.

Delilah was dying to settle the score.
She awaited with joy the belligerent bore.
She donned in his honor a topless Dior,
Sweating it out as he knocked at her door.

ACT II

As he entered the parlor he said, "Hello, toots!
Dey gave me da woid at da at'letes' kibbutz.
I jogged all da way, babe, sure did, bet your boots,
When I hoid you was willin' to again get cahoots."

"Oh, Samson, you still split infinitives, dear,
But I'll teach you grammar in bed, you big bear.
Who cares if your participles hang, Sam. Who cares?
Or your future's indefinite?" said she, debonair.

38

"And, Samson," she said, "let's put on a match.
I've wrestled with goys; I started from scratch.
I'm tops with the toehold and my headlock's a natch,
But wait till I show you my scissorhold snatch!"

And then she starts singing the joys of the spring,
When fancies are stirred, besides other things!
"My heart at your voice opens like a bird's wing,
And that isn't all, big 'king-of-the-ring'!"

When she said, "My heart opens when I hear your voice,"
Poor, dumb, stupid Samson lost all of his poise.
Standard equipment was straight Samson's choice,
So he did what he did, relaxed and rejoiced.

She said, "Tell me, my love, ere you slumber away,
Tell your Delilah where does your strength lay?
Whisper it softly, a breath, a soufflé."
"In my hair," said the dope, in sleepy dismay.

She soothed him to sleep, held him close to her breast.
When he got exhausted, she laid him to rest.
Then she ran for her scissors, the sharpest, the best;
Cut off all his hair with a kiss and caress.

When Samson awoke from his deep dream of peace,
He started to curse, to scream, and to weep.
"Who done it," he said, "while I was asleep?"
" 'Twas I," said Delilah, "you heavyweight creep!"

Many times had Delilah seen Samson undressed,
So she could have, for instance, cut hair off his chest
Or from under the arms where short hair grows best
But not crop the head of an overnight guest!

She then made a sign, a command like a queen;
Then in rushed the foe, the vile Philistines.

They grabbed poor weak Samson who stumbled, careened;
Mocked, "Show us your muscles!" then vented their spleen.

From the prison of Gaza Samson was led
By a child, while vile insults were hurled at his head.
Delilah is there with her B.C. jet set,
Screaming insults and jeers and snide epithets.

Sightless and shorn, at each break of dawn,
Samson-the-husky is grinding out corn.
Around and around, all helpless, forlorn,
He's taunted and ridiculed, scoffed at and scorned.

He pleads to Jehovah, forever in prayer,
For only his strength—never mind hair.
"Give me, O Lord, the strength so to tear
The Philistines' temple apart in the square!"

Jehovah at last heard the moans and the prayers,
So he made a dicker right then and there:
He'd get back his strength but not the long hair.
Samson praises the Lord, despite his despair.

Laughs best who laughs last, to quote a fast quip.
Samson's prayers will be answered; he was given a tip.
His power'll be restored even though he's a drip.
"I must," said Jehovah. "It's biblical script!"

As a child leads the way, we hear Samson say,
"Show me the pillars, the temple's mainstays."
He then stumbles along, distraught and distrait,
As he says to himself, "Every dog has his day."

With that he takes hold of the pillars and shouts,
"You've had it, you Philies, you phonies, you louts!"
As the pillars give way and debris falls about,
The Philistines perish, as does Samson, no doubt.

It's hard to believe this hair "doggie-do,"
So believe it or not. *Chacun à son gout.*
We know the Good Book makes mistakes (quite a few!),
Contradicts, and distorts what most prophets claim true.

All through history the women have ruled behind scene
Caesars, emperors, kings, and monarchs supreme.
They should rest on their laurels, these harlots and queens,
And shove women's lib, where it cannot be seen.

Aida

In Egypt in days when the pharaohs held sway
They made love and war in very strange ways.
They invaded and fought at the drop of the hat
Or the drop of the loincloth. Just think of that!

It so happened that during one pharaoh's regime
A maiden was captured, a princess, a dream.
She was black, that is true, but some say and do
Switch their luck by switching to that very same hue.

From Addis Ababa this Aida came,
The same as did Sheba, the Queen of great fame.
She was dragged into Egypt when her land was besieged,
And Amneris befriended her. Noblesse oblige.

Amneris is also a princess of fame;
Her dad is called King, with no other name.
That he is a pharaoh, there's no ifs or buts,
A distant relation perhaps of King Tut's.

Rhadames is a warrior, faithful and true,
Though outside of war, had a doubtful IQ.
His true love he chose from the camp of the foe;
A no-no that even a tenor should know.

The high priest is Ramfis, tough as a stake.
If you got in his hair, he was worse than a snake.
His hobby was smothering people to death,
And he'd stick around till they drew their last breath.

43

The plot was cooked up by Mariette-Bey,
A French archaeologist, renown in his day.
Then Signor Ghislanzoni and Verdi set to,
Cut, added, subtracted, till Aida came through.

The khedive of Egypt was anxious as hell
To open with fanfare the Suez Canal,
So he ordered Aida, for the opening date.
Aida arrived, but alas, much too late.

ACT I

Scene 1

The curtain goes up. We're in Memphis it seems:
A temple; the Nile in the distance is seen.
The high priest and Rhadames talk tete-à-tete.
Who shall be captain? That's for Isis to state.

When Rhad met Aida 'twas love at first sight.
She too felt the same, as two lovers might.
They sneaked behind rocks and behind the palm trees
Where they couldn't be seen if they dropped their chemise.

'Twas not quite the thing for a houseguest to do,
And Rhadames, too, was a sneak parvenue.
But Verdi got even, said, "Since you're so smart,
Sing 'Celeste Aida' right at the start."

He calls her celestial, a shapely sweetheart,
As he's planning to tear all her people apart;
He'll crown her with glory, just like a queen.
He'll give her his all, if you know what I mean.

He goes on to sing that he'll give her the sky,
A throne in the sun, no expense is too high.
With so much emotion, desire, and all that,
No wonder most tenors crack on the B flat.

While all this deceit and deception goes on,
A messenger, jogging, runs through the throng.
He announces that Thebes' been invaded and, too,
That M. F. Amonasro is planning a coup.

"My dad," sighs Aida, stifling a sob.
"Why does he come now, with the rest of those slobs?"
She's torn between love and duty, poor thing.
She's just too upset, so she starts in to sing.

"Come back crowned with glory. Give them the works."
(She wants Rhadames, not a jigaboo jerk.)
"But what am I saying?" she cries with chagrin.
"My country. My people. How can a girl win?"

Scene 2

At the Temple of Vulcan, priests gather and pray
To their idol, called Phtha, made of papier mâché.
Rhadames then gets the well-tempered sword
To conquer the enemy vile and abhorred.

ACT II

Amneris' Apartment

Amneris is squirming, lovesick on the couch,
For that guileful, deceptive, two-timing slouch.
Her wise plans are laid (so're Aida's, the slave) .
She'll fight to the finish; she rants and she raves.

Amneris' stress is cooled more or less
By the slaves that are fanning away her distress.
She then calls Aida to come to her side.
Aida's prepared for the worst, mystified.

45

"Now I must explain," says Amneris aflame.
"The captain, courageous Rhadames, was slain."
Then green-eyed with scorn, she asks, "Can you mourn?"
"Forever I'll mourn," says Aida, forlorn.

"Fie," screams Amneris. "The cat's out of the bag."
"You love him I know," she shrieks like a hag.
"But tremble, you slave, you dusky upstart.
With my very hands, I'll tear you apart!"

"Yes, you're my rival," defeated she bleats.
Thus saying, Aida starts getting cold feet.
She falls to her knees, begs, and implores
For mercy and pity; she's worse than before.

A flurry of trumpets and festive fanfare
Is heard clear and loud; cries of joy fill the air.
Amneris prepares to attend on the throne.
Aida must come; she'll throw her a bone.

Thebes Again

We are now back in Thebes, among cutthroats and thieves,
Grave robbers, mummies, priests and khedives.
The scene is all clustered with high priests and beasts,
Fan bearers, pot carriers, and mounted police.

With trumpets and horns, cymbals and drums,
The Egyptians held feasts, second to none.
Even mummies of pharaohs were dragged from the tomb.
Queens came out of closets, screaming "Jaboom."

The trombones and horns step right out of the pit,
Don diapers and helmets, and things that don't fit.
Amneris and King take their place on the throne.
Everyone is on stage; there's nobody home.

There are slaves with the braves, with torches and fans;
Banners, bidets, vessels, divans.
The corps de ballet start doing *jetés*.
With faggots to burn in braziers and trays.

In the middle of this, in a litter of gold,
Under a canopy, lost in the folds,
Is the conqueror Rhadames, lying supine,
Done up like an idol en route to a shrine.

The haughty Amneris hands him a wreath.
"That's telling 'em, baby. Right from the teeth."
She's got the illusion, she's got him for keeps,
But the Addis Ababa gal isn't asleep.

"Bring on the captives," Rhadames screams.
The basketball players rush in with their team.
Amonasro's among them, done up in a skin.
"Land sakes, that's my daddy," cries our heroine.

Her loud sotto voce is heard by them all.
"Her daddy!" they thunder, right through the hall.
Queries King, "Who are you?" to Amonasro.
"Miz Aida's dad, sure 'nuff. Dat's me, Bo.

"And look, Mr. King, you know well as I do
What happened to me coulda happen to you.
So I beg of Your Majesty, set my men free."
"Ye gods," cried out Ramfis. "How nuts can he be?"

King finally said, "Oh, let them all go.
One's quite enough; keep Amonasro.
He can stay with his daughter, Aida; that's fine.
We'll know where to find him should he get out of line."

The high priest turns pale, starts chewing his nails.
"You'll be sorry," he says as he moans and he wails.

47

"They did it before and they'll do it some more."
"So what," says King, as he starts to get sore.

He descends from the throne, says, "Please leave me alone,"
And to Rhadames says, "There's no place like home.
You fought for your land, so I give you the hand,
Of my daughter, Amneris, to rule o'er this land."

The last thing he wants is King's daughter's hand,
But he's now in a bind—a command's a command.
To escape from the wiles of this dame of the Nile
Will take some conniving, scheming, and guile.

ACT III

The Nile Scene

Night shades are falling all over the land.
From the temple come voices, muted and bland.
"Isis, mother and wife of Osiris," they pray;
Sounds rather peculiar but okay in those days.

Cleopatra, for instance, her brother did wed.
Together they ruled, until brother dropped dead.
'Twas very Egyptian to wed and to bed
Your brother or sister, so the hieroglyphs said.

These ditties were known to the high priests alone
Until thousands of years later, a guy found a stone.
It was called the Rosetta, and that was the key
To centuries of culture and sex mysteries.

Amneris and Ramfis are back on the scene.
They wish to consult with Isis it seems.
They enter the temple to pray and so on.
Amneris declares she will pray until dawn.

The Nile flows along as the Nile always does,
Murky and dull and impervious.
Meanwhile Aida sneaks on the scene
With a veil on her head, thinking she won't be seen.

Although it's quite late, she's keeping a date
To meet Rhadames and talk over their fate.
She trembles with fear that he'll give her the air
Or tell her what was WAS and end it all there.

She starts in a trance her pièce de résistance.
It's the Nile scene wherein she's afraid in advance.
Though she fears what might be, she fears more the high C.
She'll jump in the Nile if she cracks it off key.

As she plans her demise, she gets a surprise.
"Great heaven," she cries, as her father she spies.
She expected her beau, but it's that big bozo
Amonasro, her dad, the old so and so.

He starts in to curse the pharaohs and worse.
Aida, his daughter, he starts to coerce.
"I know you're in love with that whitey," he said.
"But listen here, honey, you're being misled.

"I don't trust that race; they're meaner than apes;
And your brethren and sistern is all getting raped."
Aida is shocked. She covers her face,
But the scenes of her homeland she cannot efface.

The forest primeval Aida recalls,
The temples, the vales, she was princess of all.
Her father insists that for her own country's sake
She find out the path the Egyptians will take.

In terror and woe, she answers, "No, no."
"Have pity." She begs, so he cracks her a blow.
She falls to the floor, begs, and implores.
Pleas fall on deaf ears. She can take no more.

"Have courage; he comes," he tells her and runs.
He hides behind palm trees as Rhadames comes.
Radiant with joy, the lover appears.
"Aida," he sighs. "How nice you are here."

"Don't Aida me, you phony," says she.
"You belong to Amneris," she repeats scornfully.
"I love you, Aida. Please don't get that way;
And, dear, I've an alibi. Listen, I pray."

"Oh, yes," says Aida, "that's what you think.
But remember Amneris, even you can't hoodwink.
You know how she is and how she'll vent her spleen.
And I'll be the goat, if you know what I mean.

"If you really love me, we both can be free
In dear old Ethiopia, just you and me."
"I?" he replied. "Leave my country?" He sighed.
"Live among strangers, those black, evil guys?"

"Okay, this is it, so let's call it quits."
She's got Rhadames by the perquisites.
Love must find a way. He's got to obey.
For a roll in the hay, his land he'll betray.

"What road do we take," she asks, "by the way?"
"By the gorges of Napata; let's leave right away."
"Atta boy—Napata," we hear a voice say.
If it ain't Old Man River screaming hurray.

"Here I is, Mr. Rhas'mus, I heard what you sez."
Amonasro himself steps from the abyss.
"Abyssinia forever—it won't be long now.
We both will have escorts—Ethiopians. Wow!"

"Dishonored, a traitor! Aida, for you.
Betrayer of country; ye gods, I am through."

50

Chagrined and distracted, embarrassed with shame,
"You done it," he says. "Only you are to blame."

"Traitor. Betrayer," we hear a voice scream.
It's the voice of Amneris, venting her spleen.
He's caught in the act, with his pants down—and how!
Now for sure he will land in the Memphis hoosegow.

"Run. Get away," we hear Rhadames say
To Aida and dad, who start fleeing away.
Amonasro, en route, stops only to try
To slay Miz Amneris, but his try goes awry.

ACT IV

A Hall in the Palace

In the hall of the palace, Amneris's alone,
Mad 'cause Aida, the blackbird, has flown.
She accuses the lovers of sly double takes,
But because she still loves Rhad, she'll plead for his sake.

She summons the guards to bring Rhadames.
She comforts and says, "You're sure in a mess.
If you'll listen to me, I can still be of help.
I don't have to tell you, the priests want your scalp.

"If you don't have an alibi, big boy, you're sunk,
And I'm here to tell you, you're dealing with skunks.
So do as I say, and I'll kneel and I'll pray,
And you'll come out smelling like a bouquet.

"Of course, Rhadames, you must promise you'll part
From your ebony girl friend—that two-timing tart.
You and I can be happy, this I guarantee.
You'll get out of this pickle; leave it to me.

"You don't know those birds like I do," said she.
"They're planning to smother you—take it from me.

51

So you'd better recant and try to explain
Or you'll be a dead duck. Those guys are insane."

"Why should I explain to those mummies?" he said.
"And without Aida, I'd rather be dead.
You were jealous, Amneris, right from the start;
So you had her slain, just to keep us apart."

"Okay, Rhadames. Since you turn me down flat,
Though I offered to give you my all and all that,
Aida, the snip, gave the gendarmes the slip,
And that ass Amonasro was slain—the old drip."

"So you waited till now to tell me, you witch,
Hoping I'd give my loved one the ditch.
So I'd rather, much rather, be smothered and die;
So get the message, Amneris—Good-bye."

Scorned and disdained, she lingers awhile.
For not taking no for an answer, herself she reviles.
"I did it," she says as the priest crosses the stage.
"I alone am to blame," she cries in a rage.

From the crypt in the cellar, voices arise.
Ramfis accuses, defies, and decries,
"Traitor, vile traitor, turncoat, renegade."
Rhad keeps his mouth shut all through the tirade.

The high priests and Ramfis decide he must die.
"Wretches, assassins," Amneris screams high.
And as the old mummies file through the hall,
Amneris hurls epithets to one and to all.

They ignore her insults, her screams, and her cries.
He's sentenced to death. They all wanted his hide,
Those Egyptian malfactors, corrupt, are hell-bent
To bury the guy in a coat of cement.

ACT V

Room in the Palace Hall and Prison Cell

"Aida," he moans in the tomb all alone,
As the stone slowly drops in his dread catacomb.
"May you always be happy, wherever you are.
But what's this. I feel so strange and bizarre?"

He feels being groped. No doubt it's a joke.
"In very poor taste of Isis," he mopes.
Then all of a sudden he screams in high C,
"Ye gods, it's Aida" (there on the QT).

"Don't think it was easy to slip in," she sighs.
" 'Twas a sure tour de force to slip by those guys."
She falls in his arms. They both start to sing.
"How nice it's to die. Death, where is thy sting?"

They start the duet, with blood, tears, and sweat.
"Farewell, cruel Earth. We leave sans regret."
As the stone downward slides, the skies open wide.
Two more go to heaven to live side by side.

EPILOGUE

Strange as it seems in Egyptian archives
No mention is made about smothering alive.
They were experts indeed when they sepulcherized,
So the hieroglyphs say, but they too often lied.

Pelléas and Mélisande

Of all the vapid, zany blondes,
None can compare with Mélisande.
She's brooding, aimless by a stream
Close to a fountain—off her bean.

Golaud, a hunter, dumb and strong,
Has lost his way but stumbles on.
He bumps into this flaky brat,
Who's lost but can't tell from where at!

"Hi," says he. *"Parlez-vous français?"*
"Un peu," she says; then looks away.
"Un peu is not enough," says he.
Then both blab incoherently.

It's Maeterlinck-y sure enough;
Blank verse and deep poetic stuff.
It's incoherent, vague, and terse;
But they go on from bad to verse.

She weeps because she's lost her crown
But won't permit to have it found.
She says, "If it's retrieved, I'll scream;
Or worse, I'll jump into the stream."

"Okay, okay," we hear him say.
"If that's your wish, have it your way;
But you can't stick around this spot;
Someone might come and—you know what."

She's disconnected, more than less.
Who's done her wrong's for you to guess.
"Don't touch me. Don't," we hear her say,
Although he's several feet away.

She then agrees to follow him
Back to his castle, drear and grim.
But she's enchanted with the gloom.
She loves things doleful like a tomb.

She weds her pickup on the way.
Then, nonchalant, he stops to say,
"I'm sorry I can't take you in
'Cause dad and ma are mad as sin.

"My dad is king of Allemande."
"So what? Who cares?" says Mélisande.
"Well, both my folks are snobs. Besides
They'd picked for me a blue-blood bride."

"So then why did you disobey?
Blue ribbons don't come every day.
You didn't have to marry me
And ruin an opportunity."

"I wrote a note to Pelléas;
Told him exactly how it was.
So we'll just have to wait and see
What Pelléas can do for me."

"Who's Pelléas," said Mélisande.
"My brother of whom I'm so fond.
He'll hang a lantern from his pad,
If he can fix things up with dad."

"I really don't know what you mean,"
Said Mélisande, vague and serene.

"But I'll be glad to meet your folks,
Although they do sound quite baroque."

The plot becomes still more obtuse,
With Claude Debussy on the loose.
His whole tones sometimes hit and smack;
Fall between ivories, white and black.

The transcendental counterpart
Starts where it ends, then falls apart;
Amorphous metaphysic lore;
Then Golaud starts to say some more.

"Beside we shouldn't get involved
With all those sevenths unresolved.
Full tone arpeggios sound like hell
With all those fourths that parallel."

I never heard such silly words.
If you ask me, they sound absurd.
But music always left me cold,
Even when I was two years old.

"Come on," says he. "It's getting late.
They lock the castle gate at eight.
Look, here comes Pelléas, the lamb
To meet the *fille aux cheveau de lin*."

"This, Pelléas, is Mélisande."
"Howdy," says Pellie, bored and wan.
Poor Pelléas doesn't feel right.
His boyfriend's ill; won't last the night.

Arkel comes walking down the pass
And says with spite to Pelléas,
"So's your old man sick as a dog.
So stick around," then jogs along.

Pel takes a look at Mélisande,
That evanescent, lightweight blonde.
It's surely not love at first sight;
They're both vague, like pre-Raphaelites.

But later on, down by the spring,
Mélisande's playing with her ring.
She throws it up high in the air;
It lands in the pool, way deep down there.

"What shall I say to old Golaud
When I get back to the abode?"
"Tell him the truth," says Pelléas.
"What can he do, the silly ass?"

They walk back to the castle grim,
Together—Mélisande and him.
She finds Golaud in disrepair.
His own horse kicked him, you know where.

Dear Mélisande takes care of him
With liniments and things that sting.
She wipes the blood from off his head;
Then bitter tears she starts to shed.

"Why are you weeping?" Golaud asks.
"Did you have words with Pelléas?"
"No, no, not that," she sighs and cries.
"I just feel like I'm going to die."

He gently takes her by the hand;
Then asks her, "Where's the wedding band?"
She says she lost it in a cave,
Running away from nasty waves.

"Go back and find it right away.
Take Pelléas. Do what I say.
That ring had magic powers, dumb cluck.
And if it's lost, that's your bad luck."

"Okay, I'll try to find it, sire;
But, please, stop spouting things so dire.
That stuff sounds like Rhine maidens' lore.
Rings have been lost and found before."

She sees the turret and runs upstairs;
Then suddenly lets down her hair.
Her tresses fall right to the ground,
And, boy, is Pelléas dumbfound.

His "thing" is all about long hair.
He grabs a handful then and there.
He brings the tresses to his lips,
Gets quite obscene, and almost flips.

The fate motif again is heard;
Also a motif for the birds.
Cries Mélisande, "Let go my hair
Or birds won't come back to their lairs."

They start more Maeterlinck-y chit,
Till Golaud gets a load of it.
Right then and there he smells a rat.
"Ye gods," says he, "it can't be that."

He grabs his brother by the neck
And takes him on a little trek.
He leads him to the dungeon's vaults.
About to push him in, he halts.

Then shortly after, hand-in-hand,
Come Pelléas and Mélisande.
He tells her that he's got to scram.
He got word from his sick old man.

Old Arkel, too, has ESP.
He seems to sense catastrophe;

Tells Mélisande, "You should have fun.
You're only young once, honey bun."

He kisses her, then goes his way;
Runs into Golaud—mad, distrait.
He's scratched his head against a tree
And carries on ferociously.

He wants no help from Mélisande.
He's had it from that dizzy blonde.
Asks for his sword and things like that;
Then grabs her hair in nothing flat.

Starts dragging her from here to there,
Not by her feet, but by her hair.
"I am not happy," Mellie cries.
He still drags on, despite her sighs.

He makes karate gestures wild;
Pretends he'll strangle the poor child.
He drops her then in Arkel's lap;
Says, "She's all yours, Arkel, old chap!"

As bold as brass, here's Pelléas
With Mélisande, the platium lass.
They carry on, bold as can be,
While Golaud spies behind a tree.

Golaud suspects but can't be sure;
The actual facts are quite obscure.
Too late—in fact in the last act—
He learns that Pel left Mel intact.

Debussy's school of hints and moods
Disclose the sinful and the lewd;
But without solos and sextets,
How can one know whom one begets?

This five-act lyric drama score
Gets complicated more and more.
More characters arrive; in fact,
We have a parturition act.

An obstetrician's drawing near.
The horns are sounding, dull and drear.
The midwives gather 'round the bed.
They've seen reflections in the "head."

Imagine Mélisande's surprise
When a tiny baby girl arrives.
"How very small she is," she sighs.
"She'll weep a lot before she dies!"

Then Mélisande starts to expire,
But Golaud cannot help inquire,
"Did you love Pelléas, my dear?"
"Yes," she says wanly. "Is he here?"

"Oh, please forgive me," Golaud said.
"For what?" she says, her senses dead.
"I know your pleasant camaraderie
With Pelléas was gay and free.

"I also know that he and you
Had several little rendezvous.
But just one thing I'd like to know,
Did you? Say simply yes or no."

She whispers no, her last bon mot.
She then expires in statu quo.
Alas, alack. In the last act,
Golaud learns Pel left Mel intact.

Then Arkel has some things to say.
Vapid and vague, in bass he brays

Like how he'd feel if he were God;
Then something more silly and odd.

"A life is ended," says Arkel.
"And one begins" (he's doing well) .
It must be quite profound, I think;
And no doubt so does Maeterlinck.

Methinks perhaps Monsieur Maurice
Spent too much time with birds and bees.
His humans seem to fall apart,
So evanescent. Is this Art?

Carmen

Seville is a city of love, lust, and passion.
High combs and mantillas are always in fashion.
Genteel señoritas are kept behind rails,
Guarded by *dueñas* from horny young males.

The cast iron virtue of the dames of old Spain
Was proclaimed by Cervantes and sages of fame.
But morals and customs in time and in space
Are not sacrosanct to any one race.

Take Goya Lucientes, the painter supreme,
Who agreed with La Barca that life is a dream.
And he proved without doubt that the art that conceals
Is much more exciting than the art that reveals.

To prove it, the Duchess of Alba he chose,
Who posed for him with, or without, her clothes.
La Duquesa had dare and devil-may-care,
Like Rosie, the model of Washington Square.

Comparisons are, I'm prone to admit,
Odious and snide, although some shoes fit.
And though Carmen coquetted, wiggled, and danced,
She might drop a breast but kept on her pants.

Two dames herein named both came from Spain,
Where climates are sultry and so are the dames.
So on with the story by Prosper Merimée,
Made immortal by Meilhac, Halévy, 'n' Bizet.

ACT I

A Square in Seville

We are now in Seville, on a wide thoroughfare,
On the left there's a guard house, at the right a long stairs.
The cigarette factory is not very far
Where girls roll cherotts and five-cent cigars.

A blonde ingenue, timid and scared,
Comes trembling, hesitant, down the long stairs,
Runs into Morales, and asks in a daze
If perhaps he might know where to find **Don José**.

She's told by Morales that José's on his way
To relieve the old guard, but please won't she stay?
She thanks the kind soldier but says in dismay,
"I'll return later on," then goes on her way.

Here the cigarette girls take a cigarette break;
Sing of sweet-smelling smoke as they go on the make.
With puffs, sniffs, and whiffs, they emit *la fumé,*
Blowing smoke in the eyes of the guys that might play.

It's like Spanish fly to some of those guys,
But some of the boys start rolling their eyes.
They try to act butch and sexy—*olé;*
Muy macho indeed and *también* very gay.

"Here they come," they all yell. Carmen, *la belle,*
She flies down the stairs like a bat out of hell.
Some boys crowd around, sniffing like hounds,
As Carmen seductively starts on her rounds.

She sings, "Love is a bird tameless and wild
And, like me (she sings), cannot be beguiled.

64

I may love tomorrow but surely not yet,
So be on your guard or you'll live to regret."

"*Quesque tu fais?*" with José she coquettes.
"I'm fixing a chain for my gun's epaulets."
She throws him a flower; then runs up the stairs.
It's the mystic acacia—bewitching. Beware!

He picks up the flower and says, "What a nerve.
Somehow it seems she's thrown me a curve.
The perfume is strange, heady, and rich.
And the girl? Who knows? She could be a witch."

Micäela returns, shyly seeking José.
She falters and wavers mid guards—in dismay.
She then sees José among the dragoons;
Rushes up to him frightened, ready to swoon.

She gives him the note with a few coins, and then
José sees the farmhouse, the cows, and the hens.
He'll return to the village; Micäela he'll wed;
Then looks toward the factory with a feeling of dread.

He's touched to the core; then, sighing, implores
For news of his mother, beloved and adored.
Micäela takes heart, says, timid and shy,
"She gave me a kiss to give you. Good-bye."

There's now an alarm, violent and shrill,
From the cigarette factory just over the hill.
It's a battle for fair; girls yanking at hair;
Scratching and kicking each other's derrière.

"It's Carmen," they scream. "She started the scene.
She stabbed and hit first. She's savage and mean."
Zuniga, the captain, calls Carmen "la pest,"
Has her hands tied, and prepares her arrest.

She begs Don José to help her get loose
While on the way to Seville's calaboose.
She promises thrills by the walls of Seville.
She begs him to come. She weakens his will.

As he loosens the cords, she pushes José.
He falls on his pratt. Carmen dashes away.
The collusion's exposed, reported, and then
José is arrested and thrown in the pen.

ACT II

The Tavern of Lillas Pastia

We are now in the dive where smugglers connive;
A den of iniquity where crooks and thieves thrive.
Zuniga is there, drinking vin ordinaire
With Mercédès, Frasquita, dragoons, and corsairs.

Carmen dances and sings and plays castanets
With smugglers and soldiers that gamble and bet.
She clicks with her heels as they holler *olé*.
She's the belle of the dive where scoundrels hold sway.

Zuniga tells Carmen José's left the jug,
Has just been released, so she may see his mug;
Then says, "*Hasta la vista.* I must run along.
Where's the men's room, Chiquita? And don't get me wrong."

Thereupon shouts of *viva* are heard
For the great Escamillo, the bull-slaying bird.
"*Vivat le torrero*"—the brave matador.
He's courageous and dauntless; kills bulls by the score.

He vainly struts in, pompous and proud,
Proud of his fans for crying out loud.
He describes how the bullring is flowing with gore,
How horses are gored, also brave picadors.

66

The denizens scream, delighted, entranced,
To hear how often they're gored in the pants.
Carmen shoots him a glance while acting blasé.
Escamillo she knows will be her next prey.

A voice on the way is heard; it's José,
The handsome dragoon along the pathway.
He's greeted by Carmen, contained and restrained.
She tries making him jealous with studied disdain.

She tells him she's danced for Zuniga and friends,
But she'll dance for him too, so she starts to again.
She hums as she sings and fascinates him.
Then a bugle is heard through the noise and the din.

"This is the retreat," José then explains
That he must get right back to the barracks again.
"I've danced and I've sung," Carmen says, "you dumb cluck.
And you talk of retreats. That's just my bad luck."

Carmen laughs in his face, defies him, and sneers.
"Your love is a sham or else you'd stay here.
You'd ignore the retreat," she says with conceit.
"Tell them to shove it. Remain at my feet."

Here he takes from his pocket the flower she threw
And with tears in his eyes sings Sevillian blues.
"The flower you gave me went with me to jail."
He goes on quite a bit with a long-winded tale.

"The day you escaped, kicked me, and ran,
You threw at my feet this flower so bland.
Your getaway caused such a terrible stink
That Zuniga, the fink, threw me into the clink."

"I've heard that old gag," she says. "It's not true.
If you loved me the way you say that you do,

You'd desert, join my gang of smugglers, José,
Jump with me on a horse and gallop away.

"In the mountains up there where the crooks have their lair,
You'll be free as a bird, breathing rarefied air.
Why be kicked around in that silly platoon?
Come away, Don José. Don't be a goon."

A knock at the door is heard and ignored;
No matter, Zuniga comes in, and what's more
He sees Don José, tells him, "Be on your way.
You've heard the retreat. These are orders, I say.

"Presumptuous young man, you know who I am,
So be on your way. You heard me. So scram.
And you, Carmencita, how could you," says he,
"Prefer that cheap jerk to an officer—me?"

José and Zuniga draw swords, swear, and curse.
The party gets rough; Zuniga get's worse.
The smugglers surround him and start making sport.
He gets kicked on his way, with a musket escort.

Zuniga swears vengeance as he's shoved on his way,
So the cutthroats break camp in wild disarray.
José's in a bind—won't leave Carmen behind—
So he joins the marauders; his own doom is signed.

ACT III

A Mountain Pass

José has deserted, escaped, left the troop.
He's now a *bandido,* a part of the group.
The inscrutable cassia indeed cast a spell.
Like the stars, it not only inclined, it compelled.

Repentant, the lug is now with the thugs—
Desperate, forlorn, and deeply in love.
But by now Carmen's love for José has grown cold.
"Go back to your mother," she sneers, cruel and bold.

Mercédès and Frasquita, with joy and with zeal,
Shuffle cards in suspense as to what they'll reveal.
"Love, wealth, and contentment," they cry in one breath.
Carmen shuffles and shuffles. Her cards predict death!

She shuffles again; the cards are the same.
The fates so decree, and so they proclaim.
The cards do not lie; she'll die and then he.
It's written on high. "So what," murmurs she.

The contrabandists are forced to move on.
José's left on guard as they scurry along.
He hears someone coming; fires a gun shot.
It's Micäela; she's frightened and runs off in a trot.

How Micäela got there, who can ignore,
Though in opera all's fair as in love and in war.
But she did find her way, by hook or by crook,
High up in the mountains to plead with the schnook.

José's left alone, on guard in the camp,
With orders to shoot any snooper or tramp.
When he hears someone coming, he pulls out his gat;
Shoots the brave Escamillo, right through the hat.

The shot missed his head by only a shade;
Could have ended at once his bold escapade.
He then tells José the reason he's there.
José jumps in the air; starts pulling his hair.

"Carmen?" he screams. "How dare you. She's mine.
I'll teach you a lesson, you bull-slugging swine."

69

Both pull *navajas,* shrieking curses and names.
They'll fight to the death for the wild gypsy dame.

Carmen, the temptress, arrives just in time,
Stops the combatants, kicks José's behind.
She then tells José to be on his way;
That she loves Escamillo, so, "Go 'way and stay."

Trembling with fear, Micäela appears.
Weeping, she cries into Don José's ear,
"Your mother is dying, keeps calling, 'José.'
Come leave these malfactors. Let's get on our way."

Between love and duty, José has no choice.
His heart strings are wrung by Micäela's sweet voice.
To Carmen he says, "I'll go, but beware.
You'll pay through the nose. I'll be back, slut, I swear."

She sneers at José, "Get going, you flop."
Enraged, he gives Carmen a karate chop.
She sinks to the floor, screaming curses galore,
As José, on his way, screams back, "You whore!"

ACT IV

Outside the Plaza de Toros in Seville

We are back in Seville for the thrill of the kill.
There soon will be slaughter mid shouts loud and shrill.
Here are grandees, hidalgos, señoras, señors,
Dark-eyed señoritas, and gay matadors.

They're awaiting with glee those *machos* to see
Teasing the bulls in their deaths' agony.
And some matadors tease sailors as well,
But boys will be boys, or so we hear tell!

70

But just think of the thrill when the great matador
Slits the ears of the bull to debase him some more.
Proudly he struts as the crowd yells and claps,
As he flings the bull's ears in his *novia*'s lap.

The crowd is ecstatic, awaiting the show.
Then they spot Escamillo, Carmen's new beau.
Carmencita is with him, dressed up fit to kill,
Anxious to cheer her lover's great skill.

The brave Escamillo and Carmen draw near,
Vowing true love as the mob yells and cheers.
"You'll be proud of me, Carmen," says the brave matador,
"When you see bulls and horses slain by the score."

Mercédès and Frasquita also are there.
Both rush up to Carmen and warn her—beware!
They tell her José is casing the spot.
Carmen couldn't care less. She'll tell him what's what.

As her ex-love appears, she sneers, *"Quel toupet.*
You know the score, Don José, so be on your way.
How many times must I tell you I'm through?
So get going, Casanova. I've had it with you."

She takes from her finger the ring that he gave;
Throws it at him with scorn, defiant and brave.
As she tries to escape, José bars her way.
"Carmen, you're damned." Then he goes on to say,

"I've pleaded, beseeched, begged, and implored
While you flaunt your new lover and act like a whore."
So saying, José warns Carmen, "Beware."
He then reached for his knife in grief and despair.

She sneered and she jeered and scoffed like a tart.
She defies him, so he drove the knife through her heart.

71

So shed no sad tears for this cold femme fatale.
It couldn't have happened to a worthier doll.

One can't feel too bad for Carmen's sad end.
She was warned by the cards again and again.
She might still be living had she paid some regard
To the warnings she got all the time from the cards.

LA TRAVIATA
Addio del passato

FAUST

"Ne permettrez vous pas, ma belle demoiselle?"

MADAME BUTTERFLY
Un bel dì vedremo

TOSCA

E avanti a lui tremava tutta Roma

SAMSON AND DELILAH

Mon cœur s'ouvre a ta voix

AIDA
The Nile scene

PELLÉAS AND MÉLISANDE
To the foot of the tower my tresses fall

CARMEN
Le tringles de sistres

LA BOHÈME
Che gelida manina

ENTR' ACTE
The Beautiful People

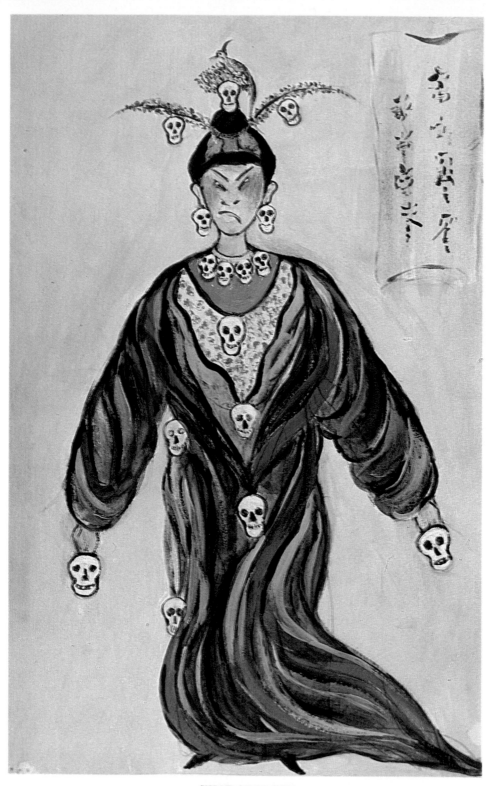

TURANDOT
Turandot, la pura

IL TROVATORE
Miserere

OTELLO
Un altro baccio

NORMA
Mira, o Norma

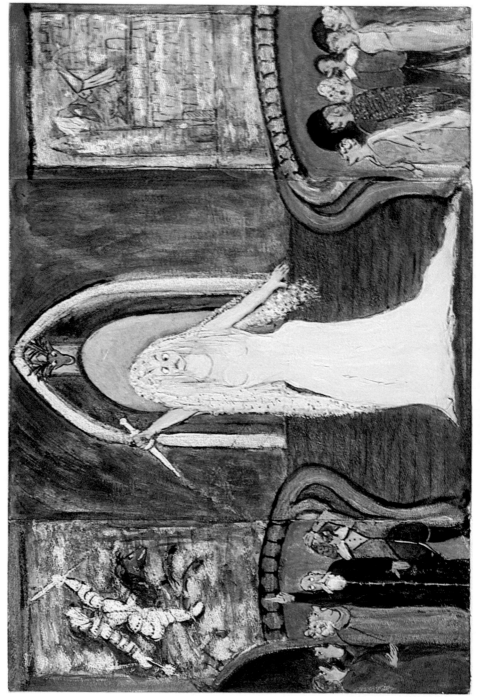

LUCIA DI LAMMERMOOR
The mad scene

THE GIRL OF THE GOLDEN WEST
Minnie at the Polka Bar

MANON LESCAUT
Manon's arrest

RIGOLETTO
Questa o quella

LA FORZA DEL DESTINO
Pace, pace, mio Dio

La Bohème

ACT I

This little gem is La Bohème
By Mürger and Puccini
About four hippies and two broads.
One's got TB; that's Mimi.

The male quartet labor and sweat
To live *la vie bohème;*
Living content, not paying rent,
And nonchalant ad nauseam.

They're *toujour* gay not *tout à fait*:
Two out of four date dames.
They stick together quite a bit.
Boys will be boys the sages say.

Rodolfo, he writes poetry.
Marcello paints red seas.
Schaunard composes melodies.
Colline writes philosophy.

It's Christmas Eve, but they should grieve
For lack of food and heat.
Rodolfo burns immortal odes
To warm his seat and feet.

And here's Schaunard, the music bard,
With dough and food and wine—the best.

'Tis said his music's fit to kill
And not to soothe the savage breast.

Now all but one leave to have fun;
The poet stays behind.
He feels a sonnet coming on
Or maybe just a rhyme.

The girls are pert. They do fancy work;
That is, in their own way.
Mimi, she does embroideries;
Musetta, well, who is to say?

As Rudolph writes into the night,
He hears a gentle knock.
"Who could it be so late?" says he.
"It's almost twelve o'clock."

Timid with fright, without a light,
Mimi stands at the door.
He greets her graciously and thinks,
"Where have I seen that face before?"

She's quite afright, also uptight.
Her candle light blew out.
What can she do, this ingenue;
She's lost her whereabouts.

She gets a light all right, all right.
She thanks him and departs.
"Ah, woe is me," she's lost her key.
We're right back from the start.

She's out of breath. She coughs, bereft;
Collapses on a chair.
He sprinkles water on her face,
With overwhelming loving care.

74

"A spot of wine?" She first declines,
Then says, "Well, just a bit."
It's love all right. Love at first sight.
What else? Of course, that's it.

"Do calm your fears. Don't worry, dear.
No doubt it's on the floor."
He finds it; hides it in his smock,
While they proceed to search some more.

And as they search, grope, and re-search,
He reaches for her hand.
And then he goes from bad to verse.
Poetic license—understand?

"Your tiny hand, so cold, so bland,
Is frozen; but let's talk of me.
My field is lyric poetry;
My goddess is Calliope.

"A *bel esprit*, a bonhomie,
That's me. That's who I am.
Now tell me all about yourself,
I beg you. Oh, please don't scram."

"*Mi chiamano* Mimi," says she,
"But really Lucy is my name.
I knit and do embroidery.
My story's brief—always the same."

"Oh, lovely maid, do not evade
Though your story may be brief.
So join the group. Give up your job.
You can apply for state relief!"

It's Christmas Eve. She starts to leave.
He begs her to remain.

He gives her tea and sympathy
And other things humane.

It's clair de lune—a night to spoon.
His passion starts to burn.
He'll take her to Café Momus
And have fun on their return.

From down the yard, they call the bard,
"The friends—the bon vivants—await.
Don't be too long. Come right along,
And if you have one, bring your date."

So arm in arm, with loving charm,
They leave the attic niche.
They're in the hall. The curtain falls.
"Amor, amor," they sing—off pitch.

ACT II

The Latin Quarter

Here artisans and charlatans
Foregather and cut loose,
Such gaity. Such camaraderie,
Especially *chez* Café Momus.

The musketeers assemble here;
That's what the four are called.
Now Mimi's added to partake
Of Latin Quarter bacchanal.

Soon on the set arrives Musette,
The parttime sweetheart of Marcel.
They've had another feud and spat,
But she's got stuff, so what the hell.

Musetta works. She does not shirk.
She also loves the baritone.
The work she does? Well, who are we
To criticize or cast a stone?

But here she comes with great aplomb
In Paris fashions àla mode.
With her old "patron," as they're called,
Which makes Marcello fume—explode.

She's mad as hell because Marcel
Pretends to see her not.
So just to catch his eyes and ears,
Her song of walking streets she starts.

With flashing eyes she attempts and tries
Her erstwhile lover to reheat.
She sings of how she wows—and how—
The hot pots as she walks the streets.

When all signs fail, she starts to wail.
"A shoe," she screams, "pinches my toe."
The old roué starts on his way
To have it stretched, the dear old beau.

With bumps and grinds, the concubine
Wins back her love, her paramour.
It may not last because of spats,
But anyway, tonight for sure.

ACT III

It's early morn, before the dawn.
A tollgate is the scene.
A tavern lies behind the gate
And custom officers are seen,

77

Warming their seats, their hands, and feet
Around a brazier center stage.
Peasants arrive with hens and eggs,
And other products pasturage.

Mimi appears, coughing, in tears.
She's begs a cop to fetch Marcel
Who's painting tavern signs for meals
And things to eat on walls, as well.

He sees Mimi, frail, fidgety.
She's had another awful spat.
And in a fit of jealousy,
Rodolfo went and left her flat.

It so appears Rudolph is here.
Marcello calls the *bon ami*.
Quick, Mimi hides behind a tree,
Where all can see her but not he.

At first the bard is rather hard;
Complains that Mimi is a flirt.
Marcel declares he's not sincere.
Then Rudy says that he's been hurt.

And then he adds she's failing fast;
Her coughing racks her slender frame.
And even if Mimi is fat,
The words are uttered just the same.

Poor Mimi hears, trembles with fear.
What can he mean? The words are dire.
She vacillates, then starts to cough,
Then in his arms again respires.

She starts a song that's rather long—
That is—only to say good-bye.

Then she decides she'll stick around
Till flowers bloom; then she must fly.

He says, "Okay. Have it your way.
At least on winter nights, we'll cling.
Then when one has to go, one goes,
Whether it's summer, fall, or spring."

ACT IV

It's now Act Four; the same decor,
As in the scene for Act One.
Rudolph is brooding for Mimi.
Marcel broods for that other bum.

Again some food changes the mood.
Two other roommates come with bags
Containing wine, herrings, and bread,
And, oh, so gay—those scalawags.

Like four gourmets they act and play,
Pretending water is champagne.
They dance quadrilles and minuets,
So fancy free, so addled brain.

The fun and sport is soon cut short.
Musetta bursts in, out of breath.
Mimi is climbing up the stairs,
Pallid and worn, of life bereft.

Mimi is led to Rudolph's bed.
She knows the way; been there before.
She's been abandoned by some guy
And yearns to see her love once more.

Mid tears and grief, to bring relief,
The friends again take things to pawn:

Musetta's earrings and a coat;
Colline even rates a song.

"Good-bye, old coat; in France, *capote*.
Again to Uncle Ben's you go.
I've never had a better friend.
How you'll be missed, you'll never know."

Then as they go, pianissimo,
Mimi calls Rudolph to her bed.
"I feigned to sleep," we hear her say,
"To be alone with you instead."

Like homing doves (that rhymes with love)
He starts to think in metaphors.
"Your frozen hands, I'll warm with mine,"
And then he goes on with some more.

The friends return with drugs and stuff,
But cruel fate, alas, too late.
The end has come for Mimi dear.
She coughs and suffocates.

A peaceful end among her friends,
Together with her dear amour.
The curtain falls. That's all there is.
There isn't any more.

Turandot

Behold Turandot, inflexible, taut,
A Chinese virago or worse, it is said.
Before one can jump in her sacrosanct bed,
One must guess three riddles or off goes his head!

To fiddle and diddle with Turandot's riddle
One must be mature and very cocksure.
A dragon is tame compared to this dame,
This almond-eyed vampire, cold, hard, and dour.

Don't think you're dealing with little Ming Toy
When you deal with this chaste Turandot.
You'll be grist to her mill, or chow mein better still.
Make one mistake, and, baby, you're caught.

Most brave defunct suitors were ardent but small,
But very well hung on the wall are the heads.
So when sex rears its head, no matter what's said,
If you can't guess her riddle, forget about bed.

Though near and akin to dear good Kwan Yin,
She's no queen of mercy; take it from me.
Cut 'em off head, no slipee in bed
If cannot solve riddle of ancient Chineee.

From far and from near came brave cavaliers
In search of delights and joy epicine;

81

Mandarins, emirs, caliphs, and peers
Greedy, but not for her Chinese cuisine.

Lao Tze, Li Po, Mei S'hing, and some more
Wrote poetry, verses, and strange lays galore;
But yet for a lay this shrew of Cathay
Made suitors guess riddles—or die at her door.

Twenty-six suitors 'tis said lost their head,
Perplexed and confused, in a quandry.
They all should have read what Confucius once said,
"No tickee, no shirtee, no laundry."

Ping, Pang, and Pong, three boys from a Tong,
Butt in and butt out, obstructing the theme
With tedious quips, facetious and flip,
Disturbing this lurid, murderous scene.

They prance and they dance and make faces.
They think they're the life of the party.
But most of the time give pain in behind,
With Chinese *commedia dell'arte*.

These three silly bores, like ambassadors,
Cajole and offend with tidings no end.
They mourn for Cathay, of eons passé,
Crying, "Mankind must vanish," again and again.

They say heads must fall, like leaves in the fall.
'Tis written in old Chinese tablets and scrolls.
The year of the mouse, the tiger, the louse
Would make the red queen want to crawl in a hole.

Ping yearns for his little gray home in the West.
The other two also grumble and stew:
Pang for his forest in gloomy T'siang;
Pong for his garden of punk and bamboo.

The blood-thirsty crowd is gay, wild, and loud.
They cry for more blood in wild ecstasy.
"Sharpen the knife," they scream with delight.
Death can be fun. Just try it and see.

A young Persian soon is led to his doom.
He failed with the riddles so now he must pay.
He curses the killer, the blood-thirsty shrew,
As the cold executioner leads him away.

A voice with a sob cries, "Help," to the mob.
It's the self-sacrificing, charitable Liù.
Her companion is old, feeble, and blind.
They have wandered for days, abused and pursued.

The venerable sire is about to expire,
Crushed by the mob. But a gallant unknown
Comes to the rescue, saves the old man,
As the rabble continues to fume and to foam.

As the prince contemplates, he's amazed, insensate.
The old guy 's familiar, but he isn't quite sure.
Then he screams out with joy. It is the old boy,
The old deposed king, his father, Timur.

Their joy is cut short. They must be on guard.
Spies and informers abound everywhere.
He begs them not to say his name and exclaims,
"Remain incognito, I warn you. Beware!"

Timur tells his son of Liù's generous soul;
How she begged for his bread; and deeds unforetold,
Like drying his tears and calming his fears.
"How nice," says the prince, bored and controlled.

Regardless of plots, the prince has the hots,
And with luck he will make the cold Peking duck.

She's hard to ensnare, this cold Frigidaire.
Let 'em all run amuck; he trusts in chuck-luck.

The blood-thirsty mob keeps screaming for blood,
When all of a sudden the Ming doll appears.
She's all gussied up with tinsel and stuff,
While the mob of the slobs falls in trembling fear.

She raises her hand from the perch where she stands,
Encouraging slaughter of heads more and more.
She warns horny studs, they'll pay with their blood,
Then proceeds with her story of horror and gore.

It occurred apropos ten centuries ago,
But never, she says, can she forgive and forget.
She's sworn a revenge, especially on men,
And that's why the wolves get what they get!

In soaring crescendo, vivace, morendo
She recalls what happened to Princess Loo Ling.
She was seized by Tartars, and a brute from afar
Raped Missy Loo Ling and did other mean things.

She stands filled with ire in her regal attire,
Erect on the balcony, poised, and serene.
She raises her hand makes a deadly command—
To avenge this daughter of heaven supreme.

The blood-thirsty mob keeps screaming for blood.
Ecstatic, the vampire responds to their cry.
All fall to the ground in terror and fear.
"Continue the carnage," she nods. "Let 'em die."

The caliph's bewitched by this dazzling witch.
All warnings he shuns, ignores, and rejects.
Although it's forbade, he'll get to her pad.
Come heaven or hell, he'll vanquish the hex.

"Okay, feisty stranger. Have it your way,"
She sneers and she jeers. "Now we'll see, you poor dope.
What's born every day and dies every night?"
In ecstatic joy, the prince says, "Hope."

In rage, fear, and scorn, the princess replies,
"Tell me, smart guy, what's like flame and not fire?"
"Blood," says the prince, without even a wince;
And here Turandot almost expires.

She steps down the stairs with scorn and despair.
The passionate prince falls on his knees.
She looks down with scorn at his masculine form,
As the mob also sinks to the ground solemnly.

Here the venerable emperor appears in the clouds.
As the mob shrieks with joy in frenzied acclaim,
"Hail, venerable Son of Heaven," they yell.
"Live ten thousand years in honor and fame."

His name is Altoum and he looks disentombed.
The old gink will be lucky if he lasts through the night.
"Live ten thousand years," the mob bellows and cheers.
In a weak voice he begs the prince to take flight.

Distraught, Turandot starts descending the stairs.
Grimly she asks, "What's like ice and not fire?"
"My fire will melt your fire—TURANDOT!"
It's correct, and again she almost expires.

"Celestial Father," she cries in despair.
"Release me. Revoke this oath, I implore.
Throw not your daughter in this stranger's arms.
Cast not a smirch on our blessed ancestors!"

"Who is this unknown?" they shriek, wild, untamed.
"His name," yells the mob, rabid, insane.

Already the prince has forbidden Timur
And also the slave girl to utter his name.

The slave girl is tortured, manhandled, and scourged.
His father is crushed by the mad hangman's heel.
The caliph looks on, unstirred and untouched,
Delighted his name has not been revealed.

Liù pleads with the prince to speak out his name.
He lends a deaf ear to her supplicant plea,
Begs her stop weeping, and go on her way.
"And by the way, Liù. Take daddy too, please."

For love, little Liù sacrifices her life,
Stabs herself in the heart, and dies at his feet.
"How nice of dear Liù not to mention my name.
The dear little thing indeed was discreet."

The frigid enchantress steps to the ground,
Grim, and determined he'll not get his way.
And although the riddles were answered and solved,
She'll fight to the end to keep him out of the hay.

He offers a deal to this woman of steel.
He'll be willing to die if she guesses his name.
The deal is a flop, so the prince, chop-chop,
Tears the veil from her face and conquers the dame.

Oh, heavenly bliss. To think what she missed,
This sinister, coy, cloisonné turtledove.
After death and destruction, torture and pain,
These two schizophrenics declare, "It is love."

And so ends the story, lurid and gory,
Of gonads and hormones, alas and alack.
But, no doubt they'll have fun, those two maniacs,
Wondering whose more impressed in and out of the sack.

Il Trovatore

PREAMBLE

Upon a day in old Biscay,
A gypsy cast a spell
On the house of Count di Luna.
And this is what befell.

They caught the hag, the gypsy bag,
And had her barbecued.
And as she turned and squirmed and burned,
These are the words she spewed.

"Go get those rats, those plutocrats.
A curse be on their heads.
Avenge me, hapless daughter. Do!"
So saying, she dropped dead.

Mid tears and pain and half insane,
The daughter stole the child
Of Count di Luna from his crib
And rushed it to the burning pile.

ACT I

In days of yore, the troubadours
Were singing columnists.
They sang of who did what to who,
And this, one never missed.

Across the moat his song would float,
Declaiming love and passion.
He vowed he'd be forever true,
As in those days was fashion.

Leonora couldn't ask for more;
Her cup spilled o'er the brim.
She rushes to her lover's arms.
Ye, gods! It isn't him.

'Twas not the swain that wooed the dame
Accompanied by his lute.
It was the son of old di Luna,
The knave, the swine, the heel, the brute.

She tells the knight, "Go fly a kite.
You're not the one. So go away."
"I'll go, proud beauty. That's okay.
But I'll slay that crooner on my way."

The rivals meet. They swear and bleat
And pledge to cremate one another.
They lose their cool, rush off to duel,
While Leonora shudders.

At sword's point they blow the joint.
They'll settle it this time.
The count draws blood; Manrico falls
But rises on the count of nine.

Wounded, he tramps back to the camp.
His wound is almost mortal.
In Azucena's arms he drops
Within the gypsy portal.

With voodoo cures, spells, and conjures,
Together with witch hazel,

They bring 'em back alive. He vows
To slay those blue-blood *azels*.

ACT II

It's now Act Two, and right on cue
You hear the anvils ringing.
And what a camp, with gypsy scamps
Singing with hammers swinging.

While anvils ring and gypsies swing,
 Azucena tells a story
Of blood and lust, of fire and dust,
And vengeance, cruel and gory.

The tale's the same, about the flame,
That broiled her ill-starred mother,
And how into the pyre she threw
Her own child, not the other.

"Then who am I and who's the guy
You threw into the pile?"
"You ask such foolish questions, Man."
I simply said, "A child."

From mouth to ear Manrico hears
The dirt that has been done.
Because Le'nor's been told he's dead,
She'll take the veil, become a nun.

"A nun? A nun? How come?" He's stunned.
He rushes to the scene
Before a novice she becomes—
A lay—or Ursuline.

Almost too late, he's at the gate.
His rival got there sooner.

Fuming about, screaming, the lout,
He'll snatch her and he'll ruin 'er.

The Count di Luna, the blackguard goon,
Is close to seizing Leonor'.
But it's too late; at any rate
The rape is off. Manrico scores.

A nunnery? Catastrophe!
Imploring litanies reach the skies.
While daggers flash and swords slash,
La Macerena saves both guys.

Man says, "You dope. Only the pope
Can free you once you're in."
"I see," says she and off they flee
To live and love, just she and him.

ACT III

Scene 1

For reasons unknown the gypsy roams
Into di Luna's bivouac.
She's spotted by old Ferrando;
Walks right into his cul-de-sac.

"What do you here?" the scoundrel jeers.
"I've seen your mug before methinks."
And as she stutters, hems, and haws,
The stinker slaps her in the clink.

"Whence come you, say?" "From old Biscay.
To seek my son, the ingrate brute,
Who left me flat, imagine that,
And left me destitute."

"Who is the dame and what's *his* name?"
"Manrico. Hers is Leonor'."

"Ye gods. The rival of di Luna!"
Here the libretto thickens more.

Then in a flash, burning with rash,
He grabs the gypsy mother;
Says, "You're the dame who in the flame,
Flung Count di Luna's brother."

Scene 2

Again the same castle in Spain;
The bridge, the moat where lovers met.
They pledge their love forever more.
L'amour toujour—but not quite yet.

He gets the news: savage abuse.
The gypsy's sentenced to the stake.
While Leonor' entreats, implores,
He rushes off to slay those rakes.

ACT IV

Prison Scene

Outside the clink ready to sink,
Leonora's on the spot.
The Miserere dirge is heard.
Manrico sings, "Forget me not."

"Forget you? Me? How could that be?
How could I e'er forget your lute
Or songs you sang that used to float
Across the mout before the rout?"

"Forget me not. Forget me not."
"Don't worry," answered Leonor'.
"I'll save you, loved one, rest assured,
My one, my own, my troubadour."

And as she cries, the count stops by.
Tears and pleas he derides, ignores.
The martinet says he regrets
He can't heap on her lover more.

Again he said, "I'll see him dead,
Lest you, Leonor', become my wife."
Alas, alack. She makes a pact.
She'll fool him yet; you bet your life.

"You've won the score, noble señor.
Now let me in that prison wall."
She'll beat him still. She takes a pill.
It's arsenic, mixed with Pentothal.

Within those prison walls, she falls
Into Manrico's arms.
She begs him flee the gallow tree;
Escape from death and the gendarme.

He starts to curse, to fume, and worse.
He's mad as all get out.
"What have you done, you faithless one,
Played hanky-panky with that lousy lout?"

But Leonora starts to implore,
"Git goin' while the goin's good."
Then on the floor she sinks once more,
Just as di Luna strides in, the hood.

"What have you done, my cherished one?"
Manrico starts the floor to pace.
He picks the fainting maiden up:
It's arsenic and black lace.

She begs him fly and starts to die,
And then we hear her say,
"I'd rather die for you, my love,
Than let that blighter get his way."

"You must not die," we hear him cry.
"Come back to life and love once more."
Then in her lover's arms she swoons.
It's curtains for Leonor'.

The count, the lout, sputters and spouts.
He's been betrayed, cheated, and duped.
"Cut off his head. Bring him back dead,
That crooning, ninny nincompoop."

As this goes on we hear a song,
Like singing in a dream.
It's Azucena's voice we hear,
Recalling days, placid, serene.

"We'll go away," we hear her say.
"Back to our mountain home."
And as she falls asleep, we hear
Her voice as she intones,

"Again one day you'll sing and play."
For hills and vales she's yearning.
"But wake me up if you see flames!"
The lady's not for burning.

In baffled rage back on the stage,
Di Luna rants and raves.
"He who laughs last, laughs best," he sneers.
"The head is off," he gloats, the knave.

The gypsy screams, wakes from her dream.
She trembles and she shudders.
"Laugh this one off, di Luna, you rat.
The victim was your brother!"

The curtain falls and that's not all.
The opera buffs all wonder.
What happens to Manrico's ma
After that awful blunder?

Otello

In Venice one day by the old Grand Canal,
In a stately palazzo that looked to the sea,
The fair Desdemona lived life a devotee
With her senator dad, a Venetian grandee.

But sooner or late', no doubt it was fate,
A black boy of mettle appeared on the scene.
His name was Otello and I'm here to tell you
He had what it takes, if you know what I mean.

Desdemona's dad was delighted and glad
To listen to stories Otello would tell;
And the blonde Desdemona, a Venetian madonna,
Was there omnipresent, an eager gazelle.

'Twas then Desdemona awoke from her coma.
Until then she was moody, snooty, and bored.
The tall tales he told them amused her no end.
She squirmed and she burned to hear more and more.

She loved all his stories, no matter how gory,
Of battles and shipwrecks and oceans and seas.
She had suitors galore, noble signors;
All were indeed of white gentility.

But Otello had stuff she could tell sure enough,
A *femme* intuition is not to be bluffed.
She knew what she wanted. What matter the hue?
As to dad, let him squirm or even get tough.

Though she acted sedate, she was anxious to date
The black boy with courage and something innate!
She counted the days, the hours, and ways
When Otello and she could indeed integrate.

She loved all his stories of combat and glory,
But of all of his stories, the ones she loved best
Were the hot bedtime stories, romantic with glory;
Kept her squirming and yearning and really hard pressed.

Not only the stories enchanted the houri.
She fell deep in love with the brave blackamoor.
So one day she fled and was secretly wed,
Unknown to her father, the choleric fathead.

When Brabantio, her dad, found it out, was he mad!
He never expected they'd do such a thing.
He fumed and he cursed Otello and, worse,
Brought Otello to court, started raising a stink.

He said in his wrath 'twas purely witchcraft;
Tried to break up the union in every which way.
But he got nowhere fast, so gave up at last,
But fought tooth and nail to the very last day.

The senate in Venice got bored with the menace;
The Turks were in Cyprus creating a mess.
So they dismissed the case against the black ace
And sent him to Cyprus to fight. SOS!

Connubial bliss was both hers and was his.
The two colors blended unblemished, and how;
So as he went to war, he asked a signor
To amuse Desdemona, then lifted a brow.

His name was Mike Cassio; he had *braggadocio*.
He was gay and serene, like a true Florentine.

"A lady's companion," sneered Iago, the fiend.
"Indeed she'll be safe with that gay Ghibelline!"

Then a friend he became to the Venetian dame,
Platonic as Plato, if you know what I mean.
But more of this later and, too, of the baiter,
Iago, the scoundrel, the villain supreme.

ACT I

Cyprus. The Fifteenth Century.

Iago, the fiend, was inhuman and mean,
A villain, a knave, a rogue, and a cheat.
He could make vermicelli out of Nick Machiavelli,
His Italian fine hand was finer complete.

Cassio he hated and abominated
'Cause Otello raised Cassio to a higher degree.
So with cunning deceit, he planned Cassio's defeat,
Got him drunk as a skunk, and chortled with glee.

He cooked up a plot involving the sot,
A duel with Montano, the stooge of the lot.
They fought and they spat in groggy combat,
Rang the bells of alarm, and other such rot.

The Moor had dispelled the Turk infidels,
Yet the mob rose in riot and acted like hell.
'Twas then that Otello jumped out of bed
With his bride at his side, Desdemona, *la belle.*

On going back to bed to Cassio he said,
"I cancel your rank, you blankety-blank.
You're drunk and what's more you created this roar.
Get out of my sight, you cheap montebank!"

Then with passion's delight, in black and in white,
A tender love scene ensued on the dock.
They returned to the castle and jumped back to bed
For more bedtime stories, and just poppycock.

ACT II

Hall of the Palace

A fiend couldn't dream a more sinister scheme,
But Iago well knew what jealousy'd do.
So with intrigue unknown three birds with a stone
He'd kill and destroy with Italian voodoo.

To his wife he then said, "Look here, knucklehead.
I want you to get me a kerchief, you hear?
Not for blowing my nose, I've plenty of those,
But this one I ask for is special," he sneered.

"It's the one that the Moor gave his high-born amour.
I love the design for reasons of mine.
I'll have the thing copied and return it, my dear.
Don't forget, it's the one with the berry design."

Then the snake in the grass that none could surpass
Went to Cassio with fraud and phony regret;
Said, "Go see Desdemona, the incarnate madonna.
Explain what has happened. She'll help you I bet."

Cassio took his advice, need not be told twice;
Begged the fair Desdemona to intercede, please!
She, of course, gave him tea and much sympathy,
And promised she'd help in his hour of need.

She then went to her spouse, told how Cassio got soused,
"And that's why he did what he did," she explained.
"And now he's chagrined and hopes to rewin
The office he lost because drink was to blame."

98

Full well Iago knew Otello's IQ;
Though a hero in war, in peace he was slow.
But Iago's fine hand needed no IBM
For calculating his nefarious blow.

With sly innuendos, andante, crescendo,
He decided to tie three in one knot.
He couldn't care less who loved, lived, or died,
Desdemona, Cassio, or the dumb Hottentot.

Desdemona, too, had a shallow IQ;
Couldn't always be sure which side was up.
She was more than naive, rather dense I believe,
So was used like a pawn by the villain corrupt.

"I like not that," said Iago, the rat,
As Cassio was leaving the Moor's habitat.
He then dropped a hint, or perhaps even two,
In the ear of Otello, and so that was that.

"One's peace of mind should not be undermined
By questioning the virtues of ladies so chaste,
Like your own charming consort and trustworthy wife.
'Twould be a pity indeed," said he, sly, double-faced.

Already a doubt was spread by the lout,
And sooner or later it would percolate
In the mind of the Moor, slowly, but sure,
Although Iago, the snake, begged Otello have faith.

"I know," said Otello to the vile, scheming fellow,
"My wife loves feasting, dancing, and fun,
But where virtue's concerned she's indeed very stern,
And one must have proof before evil is done."

"Of course, you are right," said Iago, contrite.
"However 'tis well be aware and alert.

Our Venetian ladies can sometimes be shady,
So 'tis best be aware lest one might be hurt.

"One should not condemn a fair lady, who,
When in love, did deceive her father," he sighed.
"And to think the old man said 'twas witchcraft!
But, alas, evil tongues much too oft' vilify."

He then begged the Moor be at ease and assured
That he was beloved although he was black;
So why pay attention to evil rumors;
There were plenty of whites in Venetian haystacks.

He also suggested that he wait and just see
How much pressure she'd use in Cassio's behalf.
" 'Twould be a good sign should she act clandestine,
But, of course, one mentions this thing for a laugh."

The Moor grabbed his throat and swore he'd garrote
Any friend that would falsely his wife inculpate.
"If a man steals my purse, that's trash, as you said.
So better think twice before it's too late."

'Twas then Iago said, indignant and red,
"How could you e'er doubt my integrity?"
He then said with grace, "Cassio did wipe his face
With a kerchief embroidered with red strawberries."

The Moor in despair said, "I do declare
That is the kerchief I gave to my wife.
A curse on their heads. I'll see them both dead!"
Then he rushed from the room in horror and strife.

It was here that Boito inserted the credo
Telling God off in no uncertain way.
The good bard on Av' must have turned in his grave,
Much less "lend an ear" or a nose, I would say.

It gave Iago a choice to let out his voice,
So what matter if Boito wrote in a verse.
The bard dipped quite free in Italian history,
So to steal from a thief is not really perverse.

Be that as it may, to go on with the play,
Or I might say the score, by Rugero and Joe,
By now the black Moor couldn't take any more
And went straight to the bat for a yes or a no.

Desdemona said, "Hi," as she greeted her guy.
"So what about Cassio?" the poor dumb cluck said.
Otello went grim, jumped out of his skin,
Almost turned white, went out of his head.

Said he, "Desdemona. Ah don't like de aroma.
Is you or is you not faithful to me?"
"Why, my noble lord," she said somewhat bored,
"Why not show Cassio your kind clemency?"

He called her a whore, threw her down on the floor,
Demanded she show him the hanky, then said,
"The thing is bewitched and woe to the bitch
Who lost it or made hanky-panky in bed."

She was clean out of luck, the poor blonde dumb cluck,
And it dawned on her then what Otello had said,
So instead of defending herself as she should,
She simply decided to go home and to bed.

She puffed up the pillow, sang the song of the willow,
Like the little Tom Tit, she added her bit,
Then she let down her hair, Emilia was there,
Sang an Ave Maria, and that's about it.

Like Little Bo Peep, she started counting her sheep
And fell fast asleep as strange as it seems.

Then Otello dropped in, armed to the teeth,
Kissed her twice on the brow, as she woke from her dreams.

He was madder 'n hell, called her a Jezebel,
Asked for the hanky, again and again;
Not for blowing his nose, as everyone knows,
But to make something of it. She then knew 'twas the end.

She tried to explain, again and again,
But the half-crazed Otello had made up his mind.
For her sin she must pay, there was no other way.
She must pay for her crime and must die in her prime.

So with no more to do, the poor ingenue
Was strangled and smothered, right in their bed.
Then, ah, cruel fate, too, too much, too late,
The truth was discovered, and was his face red?

Yes, murder will out, of this there's no doubt.
'Twas Emilia that roared as she dashed through the door.
She had found Desdemona breathing her last,
Smothered to death by Otello, the Moor.

"Come one and all," she shrieked through the hall.
"Otello has murdered my mistress, his bride."
With that she indicted, incited the Moor,
Though he tried to defend his foul homicide.

In bed all alone, Desdemona did moan.
"I die guiltless and faultless," she dyingly said.
Then everyone cried as she started to die,
And all just because the Moor was misled.

The handkerchief deal, Emilia revealed,
As one and all shuddered, holding their breath.
Here Iago, the rake, the scoundrel, the snake,
Stabbed the faithful Emilia, his wife, unto death.

Otello then said, "Ah sure made a mistake,
But the things Ah did hear did discombobulate.
So when you these unlucky deeds do relate,
Jes say I loved wisely, don't extenuate."

So saying he reached for his sword and he said,
"Without Desdemona I'd rather be dead."
He staggered and swooned in fear and in dread,
Plunged his sword in his heart, and fell over the bed.

Then Iago, the rake, made a dash to escape.
He was caught by the crew, restrained, and subdued.
This story 'tis said is historic and true,
Which just goes to show what a hanky can do.

So endeth with gory a black and white story.
This mortician's delight deserved a quintet.
Four deaths that we know and one more to go,
A mortal quintet that none could forget.

Norma

Norma's a play by a guy named Soumet,
Who remodeled *Medea à la français.*
He snatched the chemise from Euripides,
Without even saying, *"Permettez-moi,* please."

Then for the encore came two other signors,
Named Bellini 'n' Romani, and they both wrote the score
Of perfidious Albions, some few years B.C.,
In Merrie Olde England. How mean could they be?

In the forest primeval of Britain and Gaul,
The Druids worked magic and that isn't all!
They believed that the soul got around after death,
As they sacrificed maidens and boys at Stonehenge.

According to Caesar and his brave legionnaires,
The Druids were barb'rous, uncouth, *ordaniere.*
They performed secret rites among the oak trees.
With hoodoos and voodoos, they did as they pleased.

They were cold and indifferent, nasty and mean,
And couldn't care less if God saved a queen.
Take Norma, a priestess, for instance, yet she
Double-crossed her own Druids for a wop SOB.

ACT I

Oroveso, the chief of the Druids, appears,
Crying, "War on the Romans!" mid bravos and cheers.

105

At the rise of the moon, Norma whacks off a hunk
Of the sacrosanct mistletoe, Druidical bunk!

Norma's a priestess and daughter as well
Of the High Priest Or'veso, who's rabid as hell.
She tells the belligerents, the wild guttersnipes,
The time to attack is not yet quite ripe.

What she doesn't tell dad or the wild Druid mob
Is the fact that she married an enemy slob.
She also conceals that she broke sacred vows
And bore him two kids, but she does it somehow.

She hoodwinks the Druids with subtle mystique,
Thus saving the life of her husband (the sneak) .
She then sings a hymn to her goddess, the moon,
Praising chastity, virtue, and rays she has strewn.

She keeps flatt'ring the diva with malarkey and such,
But that loony goddess ain't gonna help much.
No matter how subtle she praises her rays,
In the end, as they say, it's the woman that pays.

The jerk Norma wed is a slick Roman heel,
A philandering Latin, a slippery eel.
For his wife and the kids he couldn't care less;
He loves Adalgisa, another priestess.

Adalgisa's a Druid vestal—and how!
The world and the flesh she renounced, took the vows.
Then Pollione appears (by the way, that's his name) .
She falls for his line, but to err is humane.

"Adalgisa," he begged, "come with me to Rome.
Why hang around with these drips 'round the throne?
I'll swear love eternal if you'll just fly away
To a civilized land. Love, live, and (oh) lay!"

106

Adalgisa, when priestess, worked magic rites, too;
Was clairvoyant and psychic, this everyone knew;
Cast horoscopes, too, for the Druids of Gaul;
Read tea leaves; and gazed into round crystal balls!

But the tea leaves and stars failed to reveal
That her proconsul wolf was a real Roman heel.
He'd break ties with Norma, his legal-wed spouse,
Leave wife, home, and children, that two-timing louse!

Give the devil his due, Adalgisa did try
To resist and reject this sly Latin guy.
Despite how she begged him to leave her and go,
"*Quo vadis,*" he asked, "in this dump all alone?"

Adalgisa knew Norma did, too, break her vow;
Kept marriage and kids a dark secret somehow.
Adalgisa confesses her guilt to her friend;
Norma absolves her and abjures help to lend.

"Do tell me," asks Norma, "the name of the guy,"
When enters Pollione, contrite, shy, and sly.
"Don't tell me it's him (or "he," as it were) !"
She started to curse, called him, "You lousy cur!

"Come away from that tree, you two-timing skunk.
You'll pay through the nose, you adulterous punk!"
Her screams, maledictions reached clear to the sky.
She then picked up a pot to clobber the guy.

He ducked just in time, then jumped, leaped, and ran,
Disgusted that Norma did not understand.
But hell hath no fury like a woman who's scorned.
By her gods she did swear he'd regret he was borned.

She continued to curse him, to scream, yell, and yak.
"He'll treat you the same if you get in the sack,

107

So be warned by my lot or you'll get what I got.
That Roman's a screwball, believe it or not!"

How could Adalgisa have known it was he,
The husband of Norma? So nonplussed was she,
She couldn't believe she had been so deceived;
Swore to give him the air. (Can this be believed?)

ACT II

Scene 1

We're in Norma's abode in the forest somewhere.
She enters with dagger, distraught, in despair.
She swore he would pay, that two-timing rat.
She'd have her revenge by slaying his brats.

Adalgisa arrives just barely in time
To stop her dear friend from committing a crime.
"If Medea could do it to Jason, that swine,
What's to stop *me?*" asks Norma, defiant, malign.

"Oh, hear me, dear Norma, pray don't be so rash.
He doesn't deserve it, that low Roman trash.
Do think it over, I beg of you, please.
Just look at those cherubs asleep by your knees!"

For Norma, these words touched her motherly heart,
Adalgisa then takes both the kids and departs.
Forsaken, rejected, Norma moans and she cries,
"I was false to my vows and for this I must die!"

Scene 2

We're back in the grove among the oak trees.
Norma's still filled with vengeance no soul can appease.
Her Virgo's conjunct with Saturn and Mars,
Which forebodes hanky-panky, said her wise avatar.

"And I thought," cries out Norma, "my chum was a brick.
But she hands me the dirty end of the stick.
That bunk about hoping to retake her vow,
That's bull and baloney. I know it, and how!"

Norma's told that Pollione is hot on the trail
Of his love Adalgisa, and this time won't fail.
He'll snatch her away from her false Druid gods
And fly back to Rome, despite all the odds.

"Oh, yeah?" cries out Norma. "That's what *he* thinks!
I'll show him what's what, that vile Roman fink!"
She flies to the altar and thrice strikes the shield,
Which means war-to-the-finish of those Roman "schlemiels."

Oroveso, the Druids, the whole mob appears,
All armed to the teeth with picks, swords, and spears.
"The altar, the gods have all been defiled."
Norma screams, "Bring Pollione and prepare the pile!"

They bring in Pollione. The Druids scream, "Boo!"
Oroveso starts raising a hullabaloo!
"Whom do I see?" cries Pollione surprised.
"Wow!" It's Norma, his mate, with fire in her eyes.

"Kill him!" the Druids scream, yell, and shriek.
Norma goes to him; then trembles, grows weak.
She offers an out to the grand prix de Rome:
"Dump Adalgisa for good and then come on home!"

"I'll pursue her," he swears, "and drag her to Rome.
I'll knock down your idol, that fraud made of stone!
Else, hand me the dagger, I'll take my own life,
But spare Adalgisa more sorrow and strife!"

"Listen," says Norma, "you vile, faithless thug.
Adalgisa will perish unpitied, you slug.

Through her I'll get even with you, have no doubt.
She'll pay for your sins, you fatheaded lout!

"She sullied the altar, the Druids, our god,
Forsook her own vows, Irmansul's sacred rod."
Norma then cries for vengeance; her final appeal.
She'll denounce the false priestess; her doom thus is sealed.

"Her name!" cries the mob, now eager for gore.
And curses upon her they shriek and they roar.
"The culprit am I!" Norma cries in dismay.
"For my crimes and dishonor, 'tis I that must pay!"

The Druids are shocked, one and all supplicate.
"Recant!" they beseech her. "Deny! Exculpate!"
She reveals she's a mother, to Oroveso, her dad;
Begs him care for her two beloved, guiltless lads.

The mob turns again and "Curses!" they cry,
And "Off with her wreath! Let the vile sinner die!"
Pollione's love is rekindled. For his sins he'll atone.
He vows he'll die with her; she'll not die alone.

Repentant, chagrined, and weary of life,
Pollione refalls in love with his wife.
Refilled with desire, he ponders the pyre.
He's yearning to burn with his spouse in the fire.

Together they step with hands holding hands
To the funeral pyre, toward the bright-flaming brands.
Our hearts break for Norma. We sob and we cry.
But flames never killed a worthier guy.

Lucia di Lammermoor

ACT I

In old Lammermoor, in the good days of yore,
The noble Scots fought and wallowed in gore.
Each other's Scotch plaids they snatched and they tore,
Clutched hand-knitted kilts, and kicked posteriors.

The Ravenswood clan and the proud Ashton kin
Were enemies, foes, through thick and through thin.
No Ravenswood dared or e'er hoped to win
A bride of Lord Ashton's sycophant kin.

Now everyone knows the old Scottish lore
Of the poor bartered bride of old Lammermoor,
Who met, by mischance, a young bachelor
Named Edgar, of Ravenswood progenitors.

'Twas love at first sight, despite feuds and war.
They pledged true devotion forever and more.
Lord Ashton found out, hit the ceiling, and swore,
Forbidding Lucia to see him once more!

But love finds a way, so the poetasters say,
And so did these lovers; they met day by day.
They met in the heather and secret pathways,
Or they kissed through the rye. Well, who is to say?

Now Norman was Lord Ashton's sly sentinel.
Whenever they met, he'd run, skip, and tell.
He scouted and spied every nook, glen, and dell,
Squealed, and made Ashton madder than hell.

111

The Ashtons were snobs, consumed with false pride.
Though bonny Lord Henry was scheming and snide,
He muddled and mixed on the Jacobite side
And was wanted in England for planned regicide.

His Nibbs then was Charlie, quite merry they say,
And when history says merry, it doesn't mean gay.
He had bastards galore. So what? Anyway,
He died with his head on. 'Twas never *coupéd*.

Henry had (you know what) caught in the sling,
And to save it he planned nefarious things.
He'd sacrifice Lucy; sing "God save the king,"
Stopping at nothing to save his own skin.

The ready-made spouse was a wealthy old creep.
His name was Lord Bucklaw and blunt like a sheep.
No matter how Lucy did sob and did weep,
She'd fare no better than Little Bo Peep.

Lord Henry got tough, raised a hullabaloo;
Said he'd cremate Edgar, that low parvenue.
Lucy fainted away, recovered, and flew
To warn and tell Edgar what Henry would do.

As she started to talk, she felt strange in the head,
The things that she said were disconnected.
She spoke of her brother with glee and with dread.
Even Ed got confused at the things that she said.

"Now calm yourself, Lucy. Just leave it to me.
I'll go to your brother, explain, and we'll see.
Take hold of yourself. You're as shaky as can be.
I'll settle that crumb. Now listen to me.

"Please understand, Lucy. I'll make no demands.
I'll go to your brother and ask for your hand."

"My hand," cried Lucia. "I don't understand.
He might chop off both. You don't know that man."

"Oh, Lucy," cried Edgar. "You're not making sense.
If I offer marriage, he has no defense.
You see what I mean? The plan is immense.
I'll pay for the wedding, at Henry's expense."

Poor balmy Lucy, she sighed and she cried.
"My brother will scratch out your hands with his eyes.
I'm the eye of his apple," she sighed and replied,
"Who said there's two sides to a story, just lied.

"So let us be sensible, Edgar, besides
Why can't I be bridesmaid, instead of a bride?
Take the horn by the bull, it's better." She sighed,
"One's often a bridesmaid and never a bride."

"Without batting an eye, he'd do sororocide.
A word to the wise is hooey," she sighed.
"By now you should know my brother's cockeyed,
So why trifle with trifles and be mortified?"

"It won't hurt to try," bonny Edgar replied.
"Why beat round the bush or the heather? Besides,
How can anyone tell? One just has to try.
I might even give him a punch in the eye."

"If at first you succeed, keep trying. Besides,
Try, try again is a silly bromide.
And he who laughs last is a silly old guy.
Better laugh first than eat humble pie."

"I do hate to mention this, Lucy, my dear,
But your whole conversation sounds loony and queer.
Go see Doc MacGregor; have a talk ear to ear.
His patients get worse, but he's very sincere."

113

"Oh, Edgar, my bonnie, don't be obsolete.
You know yourself, Edgar, the Doc's indiscreet.
He jumped from his window and died on his feet,
While a patient lay prone on the couch, on her seat."

"Well, I guess I'll be going," said Edgar at last.
"You have convinced me, my sweet bonnie lass.
I forget, did I mention I'm going to France?
So here are some letters I wrote in advance."

Edgar swore on the heads of his progenitors
That he'd send bonnie Lucy notes by the score.
But he said, "If my notes should get stuck on French shores,
I'll keep in touch, lassie, through French troubadours.

"Besides you will hear in the breezes that sigh,
On the waves of the sea, sweet messages fly.
Now I really must go, as time's flying by."
He jumped on his horse; disappeared through the rye.

ACT II

The king summoned Henry to court to come clean,
Though Hanky would rather have dealt with a queen.
Perfidious Albion—you know what I mean?
They'd switched from a queen to a king in between.

Lord Henry was deadly in Dutch as you know,
And Buck promised him he'd put in a bon mot.
He'd save Henry's neck, then said apropos,
"Don't forget bonnie Lucy, the old so and so."

As Lucy got vaguer, day in and day out,
Lord Henry got schemier fig'ring it out.
Lucy must marry that opulent lout.
"Like it or not," he started to shout.

The villain began with legerdemain,
With fast double talk, and catch-as-catch-can.
The letters Ed wrote never reached Lucy's hands.
She became more bewildered, could not understand.

By now bonny Lucy was torn to a shred.
Henry gave her a letter he'd forged, and it read:
"I thought that I loved you, but I found out instead
I'm in love with another, dear Lucy," signed Ed.

In a daze and half-crazed, she swooned to the floor,
Whereupon enters the conspirator.
"Dear Lucy," he sighed, "I've told you before.
Ed is a heel; wed Buck, I implore.

"Besides, Lucy dear, I am in a jam.
We're ruined completely, lest you wed this man.
I face a jail sentence; this is no sham.
Now be a good lass; sign this contract, my lamb.

"The contract's all set; the ink is still wet.
The guests have assembled in strict etiquette."
Lucy totters and shudders, signs her name with regret.
In rushes Edgar, *voilà*, the sextet.

Now here's blood and thunder, with sobs and with tears.
Vile threats, maledictions, shrieks splitting the ears.
Though they threaten each other mid cynical leers,
They don't move an inch, the brave cavaliers.

"Here's your ring," cries Ed, flinging a ring.
"You have shattered my faith, my very lifespring.
"And here's yours," screams Henry, as from Lucy he wrings
The gold band Ed gave her, then stomps on the thing.

They threat and rethreat, vociferous and mean.
"Let me at him," shrieks Edgar, "that Scotch Ghibelline."
While music crescendoes, they're venting their spleen.
Down comes the curtain; it's the end of the scene.

ACT III

Scene 1

The guests have assembled, all gay as can be,
Making the wedding a blithe jubilee.
They suddenly notice the two absentees
That vanished right after the "Oh, Promise Me."

"Cut out all the horseplay," we hear a voice roar.
It's Raymond, the tutor, the joy-killing bore.
Of course they stop dancing. How could they ignore
The maitre d' basso, grim, solemn, and dour?

He sings, "While eavesdropping, my ear at the door,
I heard screams and screeches and curses galore.
What was my surprise as I crashed in the door?"
"What?" sings the chorus. "The groom on the floor.

"All covered wie blood, twa surela a sight.
Wha a gift for a groom on 'is own wedding night.
Wha would gud Pastor Knox sa to see sucha fright.
A disgrace to tha church, an 'e could be right."

"Who don' it? Quick, tell us," they ask the old bass.
" 'Twa the wie lassie Lucy," he says in a daze.
"Wi his own sword she killed eem," he says to their face.
"She dina e'en geeve him a wie coup de grace!"

But what's this we see? It's balmy Lucy,
Nuts as can be singing Es above Cs;
She comes down the stairs as composed as can be,
Visualizing her bonnie from over the seas.

You have to admit, it's not easy to sit
Hearing tones she emits, while the flute in the pit
Competes with the miss, with a hit or a miss
Like a catch-as-catch-can by two antagonists.

116

Henry comes in, contrite, beholding the sight,
Is filled with remorse, knows he hasn't done right;
Also knows it's too late to change cruel fate.
The curtain comes down, but he's still full of hate.

Scene 2. The Churchyard.

Edgar waits for Lord Henry. It's pistols for two
Or, better still, swords, which they've chosen, in lieu.
While waiting for Henry, Edgar boohoos
For the dear, dear, departed, a century or two.

He stands near a hole, mournful and dole.
As he ponders his fate, he hears a bell toll.
Some mourners drop by, he asks, "Why?" and is told
That Lucia is dying, the poor, hapless soul.

They go on to tell of her forced espousal,
And why she got loony, the dear bonnie belle.
Imagine poor Edgar as they go on to tell
How her longing for him drove her pell mell.

Lord Henry, the coward, stayed home and in bed;
Forgot all about his engagement with Ed.
To that strange field of honor, he sent there instead
Old Raymond, the tutor, the old blunder head.

The toll of the bells for a soul that departs,
It's good-bye forever for Lucy, ill-starred!
"*Hout tout*, laddie boy," Raymond cries with a start,
As Ed pulls a knife which he thrusts in his heart.

Although the blood flows, he sings from said heart,
"In heaven we'll meet, love, never to part."
He has ESP and a horoscope chart.
They'll both meet in heaven, as swift as a dart.

You have noticed, I'm sure, how sinners galore,
When they die go to heaven, and what's even more,

117

Their sins are forgiven, their "shall nots" ignored.
If you don't believe me, read librettos and scores.

Only Faust, I might say, had the devil to pay.
The exception that proves what I'm trying to say:
Is that music has charm and also a way
To forget and forgive on the reckoning day.

The Girl of the Golden West

The Polka Bar. 1849.

This is a tale of muck and kale;
Of lust and raw, red liquor;
Of miners bold, who kill for gold,
Without an eyelash flicker.

Minnie's the star. She runs a bar;
Also a doggie diner.
And though men swear, kill, and ensnare,
She could not be refiner.

All tough as stakes, these mining rakes,
Steeped to their necks in sin;
Hard-boiled, uncouth, tough, vulgar sleuths,
Yet one and all love Min.

Dear Min's a virgin, chaste and pure,
And like the blessed demoiselle,
She, too, leans far across the bar,
Where whiskey, wines, and beer she sells.

She's kept her virtue in a crowd
Of crooks and thieves and Jezebels.
But in the end she gets her man,
This Gold Rush, blessed demoiselle.

A traveling minstrel wanders in
And starts to sing "Old Folks at Home."

119

Those buccaneers and racketeers
Shed maudlin tears in beer afoam.

Those yeggs that murder, shoot, and kill
Fall all apart for simpering songs
Of home and mother hard at work;
Of old dog Tray; and girls they've wronged.

Between the booze that flows profuse,
The shooting, and the lust,
Min reads the Bible to those thugs,
Though not one is abstemious.

"There is no sin," she says to them,
"That cannot find redemption,
Providing boys like you repent
Of things not fit to mention."

In spangled gowns, sluts go to town,
All painted fit to kill.
For gold they lust, cold and nonplussed,
Like that tough tart called Diamond Lil.

But that's a fact—Min's kept intact—
Has not been touched by human hands;
Until Dick Johnson came around
And stunned her with a meaning glance.

Dick Johnson is his nom de plume,
Or nom de crook, if you prefer;
A swindler come to raid and rob,
A dangerous adventurer.

Now Sheriff Rance, he's got hot pants
For Minnie, virginal and sweet;
Declares his love, by stars above;
But gets the air *tout de suite*.

Min turns him down. He spits and frowns.
"I'll get you yet, proud beauty.
My love you spurn, but I'll return";
Then goes off to his duty.

Here Dick comes in; gazes at Min.
He's startled and, what's more,
He says, "Your face is familiar.
Haven't we met some place before?

"Yes, I remember now," says Dick.
" 'Twas in the camp," he says entranced.
"Yes," blushes Min, "you *do* recall."
He's listening in, the rat, Jack Rance.

"We don't like strangers hanging 'round,
And what's your name, I'd like to know?"
"It's Johnson." "And what else?" asks Rance.
"I'm Johnson from Sacramento."

Here Rance draws back in quite a huff.
The green-eyed monster's got him down.
He sneers and jeers and sweats and fumes
And even worse now Dick's in town.

Meanwhile there is a tete-à-tete,
As Min and Johnson chat and smile.
They're getting on magnificently,
Recalling where they've met erstwhile.

The big, bad wolf butts in again;
"Look here, you, from Sacramento.
What is your business here in town?
I'm Sheriff Rance 'case you don't know."

"Lay off," says Min, "I'll vouch for him.
Now run along. Please do."

In stifled rage, Rance leaves the bar,
While Min and Johnson start anew.

And now there is a jamboree,
A hoedown right in Min's saloon.
It's heel and toe, and away they go.
He's back again, Jack Rance, the goon.

"Come on," says Dick to blushing Min.
"Let's have a dance, okay?"
And although Min has never danced,
She takes Dick's hand and sways away.

That very night Dick sees the light;
He sings of love, of June, of moon;
And then and there makes up his mind,
He will not rob Minnie's saloon.

The hour is late; Min makes a date;
Invites Dick to her little shack.
Dick's deep in love, can hardly wait
(And neither can Sheriff Jack Rance).

ACT II

Minnie's Shack

The squaw you see works for Minnie.
From Gitche Gumee, Wowkle came;
An unwed mother, with papoose;
Billy's the unwed father's name.

They slouch around phlegmatically,
With little more than grunts and ughs;
But decent Min has seen to it,
Her betrayed maid will wed that mug.

Min starts to tidy up the joint.
She's all keyed up to make the scene.
She puts away her little gun;
Then tries to look calm and serene.

She knows a gun's a girl's best friend.
Diamonds can leave one in the lurch
In case some jerk attempts to rape—
Or even worse—to snatch a purse.

She sticks some roses in her hair;
Then has the table set for two.
One way to get a man 'tis said
Is by the stomach, and it's true.

Oh, joy supreme. He's here, her dream.
He starts to clutch and steal a kiss.
She never has been kissed before,
So says, "No, no!" with emphasis.

She never has been kissed, says she,
And then she starts a yarn to tell;
Goes on to say, and this a quote,
"Give a man an inch, he'll take an ell."

These sentiments are in the script;
Libretto written by some drip
Who wrote that touching sentiment;
Enough to give a guy the pip.

"What a nice, cozy room," says Dick.
"Oh, do you like it?" replies Min.
"Everything in it is like you."
The furniture appeals to him.

She then goes on about her pintos
In *allegro vivace* and *lirico spinto*:
How they gallop through fields beyond the hills;
Then how in the mountains they go galloping into.

As more of this slush and gush goes on,
A storm arises, threat'ning and grim.
Thunder and lightning, hail and snow;
Not fit for a man or beast, least him.

The gentle crook says he must go.
How could he stay and compromise
This well-bred barmaid, pure as snow?
'Twould be a mistake; not very wise.

But Minnie cannot let Dick go,
So as he started to leave, she said,
"Your thoughtfulness quite touches me."
So graciously offers him her bed.

"It's madness to go out tonight;
Insane to venture out of doors.
You take my bed, I beg of you, Dick.
I've slept upon the floor before."

She begs him please to acquiesce.
"Talk through the curtains. Be my guest."
Behind the wardrobe she then goes,
Puts on her nightie with finesse.

She settles down before the grate,
Says goodnight from the floor.
The hanging curtains separate;
Virtuousness could do no more.

They settle down, sweet and discreet.
But what's this noise, this awful roar?
Loud talking, screaming oaths,
Rance and his gang burst through the door.

Crash on the scene the sheriff mean
Arrives, and with the fuzz,
He stomps and screams with words obscene,
Tells Min who Johnson is and was.

Right after Jack has left the shack,
Our Minnie now is mad as hell.
She lets Dick have it then and there;
And stops him when he tries to tell

Of how he got the way he is.
He blames it all upon his dad;
A desperado from a gang
Of tough *bandidos, mucho* bad.

His poor, dear ma left destitute,
Without centavos, poor, bereft;
So it was up to him—who else?—
To keep them from starving to death.

But when he met our darling Min,
He vowed from then he would go straight;
But nemesis caught up to him,
And now he fears it is too late.

She's mad, so she calls Dick a cad,
A double-dealing so-and-so.
She throws him out and slams the door;
Screams, "Don't come back, Lothario!"

Poor Min thinks she is through with him,
And as he's taking flight afright,
A shot is heard—they've got their bird.
Dick stumbles back, wounded in flight.

Desperate and sore, Minnie deplores
What's happened to her darling Dick.
She hides her wounded love upstairs;
Then slugs it out with Rance, but quick.

Rance has come back to Minnie's shack.
He sneers and jeers, "I know he's here.

I fired a shot and hit that mug."
Min laughs and says, "You're wrong, Jack dear."

"Cut out that 'Jack,' I'm Sheriff Rance.
I'm here on duty bound.
In case I'm wrong, I'll run along,
But swear I'll get that greaser hound!"

"Well, look around until he's found.
Go search my pad. Besides, you're mad."
"You said it, babe. It's you I crave."
He grabs and smothers her, the cad.

"I'm hot as hell, my haughty belle."
She struggles; wrenches herself free.
He chases her around the joint,
Breathes hard with sexuality.

Min grabs a bottle which she swings,
Her cast iron virtue to defend.
And as the lecher fumes and pants,
A drop of blood falls on his hand.

It droppeth like a gentle rain,
From up above where Dick is at.
And who says mercy is not strained?
It is when dealing with a rat!

She takes a chance with Sheriff Rance.
She offers to him a deal.
A game of poker will decide.
If Rance wins, Dick's fate is sealed.

So Sheriff Rance, he sees his chance
To dicker with proud Min.
I lose, you win, the deal is grim.
She sneers, "Now I'll show him."

She takes a pack right off the rack.
Two cards slip in her sock.
They start the game, and who's to blame
If she outsmarts the fox?

She cheats and wins (that's telling him).
He's lost his prey at cards.
"Get on your way," we hear her say,
"Go join your blasted avant guards."

With love and prayer and loving care,
She brings Dick back alive.
"Escape, my love," we hear her say,
"Before the pigs arrive."

But it's too late; the deviate
Is caught by Rance's gang.
This time he'll see the gallow tree;
He'll swing, he'll dance, he'll hang.

"Go say farewell to your gazelle,"
They yell, "then on your way.
You've had it, Dick, you greasy hick;
Your doom is sealed today."

"Okay," they shove him on his way;
"No foolin', you'll get strung.
You can't get loose—try—on this noose;
You renegade, you crook, you bum."

He says, "I care not if I live or die.
Unloose me and I'll slit my neck.
But one last wish I beg you'll grant.
Tell Min my love is true, by heck.

"I'd like to say or write a lay,
Like sonnets from the Portuguese.

But poems are made by fools like he
That wrote that hogwash 'bout a tree.

"But since you're bound to hurry me,
Please tell Min that I'm safe and free;
That no one did I love but she;
Then hang me on that goddamn tree!"

Here Rance jumps up, afire with ire.
He wants to punch Dick in the eye.
Those worthies hold him back by force.
Rance says, "Two minutes; then you die."

But lend an ear. What's this we hear?
It's Minnie with her colt;
Then jumping off her horse's back,
She tells them all to bolt.

She tells these thugs, these hardboiled mugs,
"Enough, you lousy rats, enough!
Is this the way you all repay
The whiskey you got on the cuff?

"And that ain't all, you mugs who brawl,
Slug, swindle, fleece, and cheat;
I'll shoot and kill the first that moves."
She's armed up to the teeth.

They cringe and sigh, then by and by
They do not act so tough and rough.
They soon get wise; they compromise;
They're diamonds in the rough.

They cut Dick loose; take off the noose;
Give up the lynching and the strife.
Min falls into her lover's arms;
He's stuck with her for life.

"Farewell," they say. "Have a nice day."
The sleighing has been rough and hard.
Dick's glad to leave with all his parts
And miss the fate of Abelard.

They take the old Sierra trail,
Dick and our Min, so debonaire.
She's kept her virtue to the end,
When all around were losing theirs.

In baffled rage Rance slinks away.
He's mad as all get out.
Not only did he lose his prey,
He's lost the girl, the lousy lout.

Thus ends the opus of the West,
Of hardboiled thugs and mining meanies.
It also ends the wear and tear
Of Dave Belasco and Puccini.

Manon Lescaut

This tale of unrequited love
Was written by an abbé;
A simple nuncio of the cloth,
Though with much sexy savvy.

As through the saintly halls he strolled
Reading his breviary,
His thoughts were not all scriptural,
Despite the monastery.

The *bon curé*, I do dare say,
Before he took the chastely vows,
Like Augustine made hot forays
And has hangovers now.

When human passions stirred the breast
And fleshpots spilled to Tartarus
Repentant sinners became saints
At home or strolling toward Damascus.

However be that as it may,
This is Manon Lescaut.
Italians say her cognomen
To rhyme with fought and caught and bought.

ACT I

This act takes place in old Amiens
Where *frère* and *soeur* Lescaut arrive

Upon a coach shared by a guy,
A hoary fox with youthful drive.

The brother of Manon's a heel,
Corrupt, debauched, and dissolute.
He plans to sell his flesh and blood
To a galoot, while still en route.

Returning to a nunnery
To brush up on a thing or two,
The stagecoach stops before an inn.
'Tis there she runs into Des Grieux.

Des Grieux tells students such a dame
He'd never seen, and what is more,
If Helen launched a thousand ships,
This face would launch a man-o-war.

Lescaut, the crook, and the roué
Inside the inn discuss the fee.
It's cut and dried and bona fide;
She'll be delivered COD.

Edmondo, staunch friend of Des Grieux,
With students that frequent the inn
Has overheard the shanghai scheme,
Draws near Des Grieux, and cautions him.

The chevalier, without delay,
Accosts the charming demoiselle.
"Pray tell me, gracious maiden, do.
What is your name, I beg do tell?"

"Manon Lescaut," she sadly sighs.
"Alas, poor me, I'm on my way,
Back to the convent I must go;
My parents' wish, kind chevalier."

132

The chevalier without delay
Informs Manon about the plot.
She swoons, falls in his arms, and begs
For he, himself, her to abduct.

They jump into the cabriolet
That's waiting just outside the inn.
They speed away to gay Paree;
Love found a way for her and him.

As the old beau and rake Lescaut
Come to the inn, they're stupified
To see the lovers taking flight;
The old futz's furious, contrite.

The so-and-so brother, Lescaut,
Consoles the lecher with tact,
Entreats him to rely on him,
To get Manon into his sack.

The sages say, and who'd gainsay,
That love's a many splendored thing.
But who can ignore the wolf at the door
When landlords and tradesmen knock and ring?

Yet poor Manon did carry on
With tea for two in a sleazy pad.
But she longed for the things that money can buy;
Things she'd dreamed of but never had.

How could she know unless she'd go
To Athens, Cairo, or to Rome
Whether or not the poet lied
Who said there was no place like home?

So one fine day she stole away,
With crook, Lescaut, the scheming rat.

Without a word or farewell note,
She ups and leaves her lover—flat.

Jilted, abandoned, poor Des Grieux
Pulls out his hair, declares, forswears
The world, the flesh, devil-may-care.
He'll take the vows. He's through. So there!

ACT II

In eighteenth-century opulence
Manon's the old man's turtledove.
The old roué did get his way,
Which proves that money can buy love.

The creaky beau, in his own way,
Worked overtime to charm his pet.
But haute couture admiring guests
Failed to amuse the blithe coquette.

The madrigals and minuets
Got on her nerves, made her depressed;
So did the dancing lessons, too,
The flattery, and all the rest.

The silken sheets, the gold alcove
Could not dispel the deadly bore.
She longed for more vivacious things,
Like shuttlecock and battledore.

Oh, how she missed the chevalier,
Wept when she heard he'd taken the vows.
So just imagine her delight
When he arrived with sly Lescaut.

Lescaut, the double-dealing rat,
Is in the act once again; once more.
He told Des Grieux where Manon's at
And led him to her very door.

A lovers' quarrel thereon ensues;
The chevalier enraged is he,
Then once again becomes enthralled,
Falls for Manon's fiddle-de-dee.

They fall into each other's arms,
Embracing, swear *l'amour toujour.*
She'll leave the gilded cage *tout de suite,*
Though miss the luxury, for sure.

While in her lover's arms she lies,
The ancient Beau Brummel appears.
His face is red. He swears revenge.
He'll call the cops, the brigadiers.

"What graciousness, Madamoiselle.
How touching is your gratitude
Within my very walls betrayed.
What charming maiden turpitude."

"Why not, you fumbling 'ristocrat,
You creaky, creepy carapace.
Take a good look," she sneered and held
A shining mirror to his face.

"*Merci beaucoup,* Mademoiselle,
No doubt you prefer bread to cake."
Then, bowing low in baffled rage,
Said, "*Au revoir,* Miss Rattlesnake."

Lescaut, the racketeer, the crook,
Breathless, he crashes through the door.
They've been denounced, he warns the pair,
Then rushes toward the corridor.

"Git goin'. Quick. Split. On your way.
They're near the porte-cochère. Beware.
No time to lose. Be on your way.
Follow me down the servants' stairs.

"Don't hesitate. Breakout. Escape.
You face imprisonment, exile.
I got it from the horse's mouth
Down at the barracks. Quick. Defile."

The guards arrive and case the joint.
It's now a case of touch and go.
The flighty Manon loots armoires,
The Louis Quince and Rococo.

She makes a haul of precious gems,
Which she conceals between her cape.
She's nabbed; the gems spill to the floor;
She's blocked attempting to escape.

The broken-hearted chevalier
Will share her fate for woe or wiel.
He swears he'll follow his Manon
Who's on her way to the Bastille.

ACT III

Le Havre

Le Havre, the sea, the boat, a shack,
A gate, a guardhouse bleak and bare;
A barrack with projecting bars,
This is Manon's last pied-à-terre.

Lescaut points out the bribed gendarme
As he taps lightly on the bars.
A window opens; there's Manon,
As lovely as the evening star.

Des Grieux runs to the old caboose
As Manon stretches out her hands.
Between the bars, he kisses them;
Again they're both in Disneyland.

"You'll soon be free, my love," says he.
"Together we will flee this dump.
We've bribed that crummy racketeer,
Your brother's phony aide-de-camp."

Des Grieux is jittery just the same,
Distraught, uptight, distracted, taut.
Foreboding fears assail his mind.
He fears the deal will come to naught.

His premonitions were not wrong;
The planned escape has been betrayed.
A shot is fired. The jig is up.
Again another egg's been laid.

Her evil star is still bizarre.
Saturn and Mars still dog her heels.
They'll not relent; they'll get her yet.
No wedding bells for her will peal.

Meanwhile the tarts are rounded up.
The sergeant's told to call the roll:
Ninette, Ninon, Manon, Clarette,
And many others, brash and bold.

"Git goin', chicks," the sergeant says.
"Go ply your trade in southern climes,
Where men are men and freely spend.
Besides, you'll have a whooping time.

"You won't be *hors de combat* long;
Those sultry gents all rare to go.
You'll make it rich, you go-go dames,
So skip along on the bateau."

Some march along with *je m'en fiche*,
While others scoff, snort, sneer, and jeer.

137

Manon, in tears, sighs a farewell
To her despairing chevalier.

The chevalier pleads in dismay.
He kneels; he begs *le capitaine*
To take him on—noblesse oblige.
He says, "Okay. On Board, brave man."

Oh, joy supreme; bliss unforeseen;
Togetherness, to sink or swim.
Manon resays, "Love found a way."
They're reunited, her and him.

ACT IV

A Plain in Louisiana

The man-o-war pitched, rocked, and rolled.
All hands aboard swoon overwrought.
They landed, more dead than alive,
With Jacobins and Sans Culottes.

In days gone by in Louisianne,
The French dumped there their rank and file.
No boulevardiers anxious to play,
Only lascivious crocodiles.

Manon grew weary day by day,
Disheartened, cast off, woebegone.
No Vieux Carré in them there days;
And much less dinner at Antoines.

Exhausted, fainting, worn, athirst,
Helpless they strayed through swamps and bogs.
No one to lend a helping hand;
No sign of life, just croaking frogs.

Manon grew feverish, worn, and spent.
She's reached the point of no return.

The heat, the bayous, gnats, and fleas;
This is the end of her sojourn.

The chevalier is torn, bereft;
Finds for Manon a place to rest
As he seeks shelter, water, help.
It's all in vain; an empty quest.

"Alone. Abandoned. Lost," she sings,
Wishing she'd not been what she's been.
She prays forgiveness for her sins;
One more repentant Magdalen.

The shadows fall. The sun has set.
Her time is up. She's on her way.
The chevalier comes back in time
Her tears and fears to soothe, allay.

Her eyes and nose are lacrimose,
A very touching mournful scene—
A kiss—the last. He's in despair.
She dies near dear old New Orleans.

Rigoletto

Mantua. Sixteenth Century.

This could be a saga of the wily Gonzagas,
Those dissolute, profligate, foul libertines,
Who back in Mantua, Ferrara, 'n' Padua
Kidnapped and slayed in a fashion obscene.

The Borgias had orgias, depraved, wild, and gorgeous.
The de Medicis too lived it up with their popes.
They kicked up their heels in red copes trimmed with seal.
But for virgins in Mantua there was no hope.

ACT I

Scene 1

Not even a gaucho could have been more macho
Than Gualtier Maldé, the duke, as you'll see.
After doing girls wrong, he'd burst into song,
Singing "Women are fickle," the debauched licensee.

The women he found could be all pushed around,
So he shoved them on couches, sofas, and beds.
He abducted, seduced, Monterone's *jeune fille,*
And the sly Rigoletto laughed off his head.

"Laugh, you old rake, you poisonous snake,"
Cried Monterone, a father bereft.

"I curse you, vile serpent. Blood be on your head."
With this malediction, old Monterone left.

Shocked, stunned, and appalled, consumed in his gall,
The court jester's leer froze on his face;
Perplexed, at a loss, made the sign of the cross,
Then solemnly left, in a slow, measured pace.

The courtiers held sway in a court foul and gay,
Deceitful, intriguing, the Renaissance way;
Making dates on the sly, with dames that comply,
Not giving a fig who's deceived or betrayed.

The Duke is eclectic and not too selective.
He couldn't care less whom he got in his lair.
He sings, "She or she, makes no difference to me,
And the wrath of duped husbands is not my affair."

Rigoletto grows worse, brooding over the curse
Hurled at his head by the Count Monterone.
He worries and frets for his daughter, his pet,
Who lives with a daft, irresponsible crone.

As he mopes like a churl o'er the fate of his girl,
He's approached by a brigand, a killer, a thug.
He stops Rigoletto in front of his house,
Whispers, "Be on your guard, you're surrounded by mugs.

"I'm Sparafucile, better known as the heel.
I liberate folks from whoever it be.
I save, for a price, folks from danger and strife.
I deliver a creep, defunct, COD.

"I've a beautiful sister; no man can resist her.
She gives me a hand to lure men, understand?
I might add if perchance, you've no cash on hand,
We'll bump someone off on the installment plan."

"So you work with your gun," said the jester. "What fun!
My weapon's my tongue, more potent, you bum.
Leave your name and address, and in case I'm harassed,
I'll give you a call, you Burgundian scum!"

Scene 2. Rigoletto's Dwelling.

After leaving the louse, he enters his house.
Gilda flies to his arms with cadenzas galore,
Then with more *fioriture*, staccato, bravuras,
She asks her dad questions he more than deplores.

"Speak, daddy, do, just one word or two.
Tell me vis-à-vis about our family tree.
I know it's a subject that pains you indeed,
But I'd like to know who mother was, please."

"I'd rather not say, at least not today.
Speak not of that, angel, but let's just chat."
Then avoiding all questions about pedigree,
He tells her her mother is dead and that's that.

Still obsessed by the curse, he speaks to the nurse,
The zany Giovanna, a slim chaperone.
"Watch over this flower (his Gilda he means) .
If anyone knocks, say there's nobody home."

Gilda then tells her dad she's contented and glad,
So she goes straight to church after leaving the house,
But she did not confess that she met after mass
A student, who said he was poor as a mouse.

"Gracious maid," said the guy, the wolf in disguise,
"Allow if I may, present myself, pray.
I'm a poor, humble student. I'm Gualtier Maldé.
Please, may I walk you home? I'm going your way."

143

The gullible Gilda accepts with delight.
In the courtyard the duke swears love evermore.
Ecstatic, enraptured, she falls for his line
Then tells him to scram, the old man's near the door.

She was touched to the heart by the lying upstart
Who gave modest Gilda a false nom de plume.
But what's in a name when a guy smells a dame,
And a dame to a wolf smells like roses in June?

"*Caro nome,*" she sings; with *bel canto* it rings.
She could not efface the name from her head;
She trilled like a bird, every phrase, every word;
Then picked up her lantern and went straight to bed.

We are still in the road where Gilda abodes,
And what's this we see, courtiers by the score.
They plan to abduct for a joke and a laugh
The gal they suspect is the old jester's whore.

Here the plot thickens, and thickens some more,
But in opera all's fair as in love and in war,
And none take offense, if things don't make sense;
The show must go on; it's theatrical lore.

Rigoletto appears and starts trembling with fear
As he finds the courtiers in front of his house.
But they deftly explain that they're playing a game
To abduct from next door their own comrade's spouse.

With masks and with cloaks for this practical joke,
The nefarious group set to work on the task.
"Let me in on the spree," says the jester in glee.
"And since you're all disguised, give me, too, a mask."

It's hard to believe, he could be so deceived,
But this plot is chuck full of such tommyrot.

They convince the poor dolt, the ladder to hold.
(This is Piave's libretto, believe it or not.)

The kidnap takes place, sardonic and base.
Mid screams of despair, away Gilda's led.
For bad or for worse, Old Monterone's curse
Relentlessly falls on the old jester's head.

ACT II

Hall in the Palace

The heartless courtiers, unscrupulous peers,
Concealed in the palace the abducted girl,
Derided the clown, pushed and kicked him around,
Rigoletto's despair was a laugh in their world.

With a smile on each face, the rakes sought His Grace;
Told the duke they'd abducted the old jester's broad.
"We'd suspected the jester of hiding a love,
A benign concubine," laughed the conspirators.

The duke smelled a rat; thought could it be that
His jolly courtiers had made a mistake;
That he'd find in his lair the maiden so fair,
Gilda, his prey? Oh, boy. What a break.

When the scheming young duke discovered the fluke
And found he'd been duped by his own sycophants,
He stopped being jocose, said they'd pay through the nose;
He'd give all those jokers a kick in the pants.

He seeks and he finds his love in a bind,
Concealed in the palace, misused and rebuked.
She falls in his arms in tears and alarm.
She then is seduced by the inconstant duke.

Needless to say, the duke got his way.
She gave him her all with love in her heart.
It's a *femmes* whole existence, the sages do say.
It was fiddle-de-dee with the duke from the start.

Disheveled, dismayed, seduced, and betrayed,
Gilda rushes and drops at the old jester's feet;
Then in misery and pain confesses her shame,
As he comforts his daughter in anguished defeat.

In frenzied despair, pulling his hair,
The heart-broken jester starts playing it cool,
Concealing his pain, pretending a game,
Does a "laugh, clown, laugh" act in a cold court of fools.

As he gets nowhere fast, he breaks down at last.
With sobs and with tears, he pleads all in vain.
"Where have you hidden my pride and my joy?"
They ridicule, taunt him, again and again.

Monterone reappears under guard, and he sneers
As he points at the portrait that hangs on the wall.
"Though I cursed you, vile duke, you live after all.
Your sins go unpunished; you live after all."

"Old man, you are wrong, and it will not be long.
You'll soon be avenged," the jester replies.
Then addressing the portrait, he vents out his spleen.
"Vendetta, tremenda vendetta," he cries.

ACT III

Sparafucile's Duplex

The jester's hell-bent to avenge with revenge
His daughter, betrayed by His Highness, the skunk.
He'll pay with his life, with the thrust of a knife,
And die like a fly, the philandering punk.

146

Although Gilda mopes over the dope,
She can't be convinced her lover's a heel.
Rigoletto will prove that the duke is a churl.
A scoundrel, deceiver, a slippery eel.

The deal has been made; the killer half paid.
The seducing malfactor will get what he gets.
The evening is rife with murder and strife,
With nothing in sight but the thrilling quartet.

They arrive in despair at the crook's pied-à-terre.
Gilda is led to the murderer's lair.
She trembles with fear. She listens and hears
"*La donna è mobile,*" that old hackneyed air.

Imagine that chaser, that woman debaser
Singing, "Women are fickle," that lecherous rat.
Who's more mobile than he, smelling fire plugs and trees;
That wolf in brocades, that debauched plutocrat.

"Come here, Gilda dear. Lend an eye and an ear.
Stand here and listen and look through the crack."
In terror and fear she looks and she hears
That mundane seducer, that sex maniac.

Maddalena, the slut, accustomed to smut,
Kids the duke, more or less, but falls for his rot.
Believe it or not she's touched to the heart,
Or rather he touched a more vulnerable spot.

She fell for the swine hook, sinker, and line,
Begged her brother, the killer, to spare the signor.
The assassin agrees, in terms such as these,
To kill the first man that knocks at their door.

Gilda heard what they said, and although her heart bled,
She'll give up her life for the man she adores.

147

She was glad daddy dear was not near to hear
The evil complot of the crook and the whore.

To Gilda the father said, "Go on ahead.
Get a horse and return disguised as a man.
When my task is complete, we'll blow this retreat
And rush to Verona as fast as we can."

Attired in men's clothes, as a metamorphose,
Gilda quickly returns to the murderer's shack.
She knocks quite discreet, softly says, "Trick or treat?"
They open the door and she's stabbed in the back.

Rigoletto returns to settle the terms;
Paid the rest of the dough to the murdering thief;
Took the sack on his back, ecstatic with joy;
Contented starts off with revengeful relief.

"Do please allow me," said the killer with glee,
"To throw the sack in the river. Our aim is to please.
We call and deliver, right into the river.
I'll throw the sack in with pleasure and ease."

With joy and dispatch, the clown opens the sack,
"Ye gods. Am I mad? I'm losing my head."
He discovers his Gilda, breathing her last,
Mortally stabbed by the killer who fled.

"Oh, Gilda, my loved one," he moans and he cries
As Gilda reacts and sings from the sack,
"In heaven with mamma, we'll pray for you, dear."
With that she expired, alas and alack.

Somehow Gilda knows to heaven she'll go,
Meet mamma and pray until papa gets there.
And though Gilda is dumb, naive, and then some,
The Piave libretto is a pain, you know where.

La Forza del Destino

In the Castle of the Marquis of Calatrava near Seville

The march of fate, treason and hate would make the Greeks'
    Euripides
Turn green with rage and jealousy, and so I think would
    Sophocles.
The hand of destiny and doom, believe in this or not,
Will make you guess, suspect, surmise, just who did what to
    whom—for what?

The strong arm of coincidence is stretched beyond repair;
There's blood and thunder, cold revenge, and cloaks and
    daggers everywhere.
If without doubt you figure out what this frenetic play's about,
You'll be at home with Sherlock Holmes, and even Sigmund
    Freud, no doubt.

In the first act, not based on fact, we hear the Marquis say good
    night
To Leonore, whom he adores, his loving child, his heart's
    delight.
While on his way to bed he says, "I'm happy, Leonore, that
You gave the gate, before too late, to that half-breed Inca rat."

But sex is many a wondrous thing, despite the ties that bind,
And Leonore plans to elope, leave home, Papa and all, behind.
The Señorita fell in love with this *muchacho* from Peru,
But the Marquis is adamant; to him all Incas are taboo.

149

As time goes by, she starts to cry, "How can I leave my genitor?
What will I do in far Peru, away from home that I adore?"
Her faithful maid says, "What the hell, you know the old man's
    adamant.
So let's get goin', Leonore, and can that 'home sweet home'
    lament."

The half-breed Inca from Peru jumps from the balcony on cue.
The two embrace. "Let's blow the place," so says the Inca
    parvenue.
"Come, come, my sweet, don't get cold feet, *mi dulce amor, mi
    corazon.*
It's getting late, don't tempt the fates; let's get away, *vamos,*
    come on.

"Time marches on, *mi corazon,* let's make it while we can."
They hesitate, now it's too late, there's the Hidalgo, sword in
    hand.
"Seducer brash, I'll cook your hash; you'll die," says the
    enraged Marquis,
While Leonore starts to implore her dad in tears and bended
    knees.

The Inca bares his chest and says, "Okay, strike, noble sire."
"I wouldn't soil my hands, half-breed," says the Marquis with
    scorn and ire.
"Go grab him, servants, by the arse, he isn't worth the
    coup de grâce."
'Tis then Alvaro grabs his gun, just as the servants cringe and
    run.

"Your daughter, noble sire," says he, "is just as pure as was
    Marie.
" 'Tis I alone who am to blame, unheeding the amenities.
So take my life if you desire, and let me at your feet expire."
The pistol he threw on the floor—went off, and killed the noble
    sire.

150

The kitchen crew and hired help ran in to see what's all about.
"Who done it, who?" they scream and shout. "No doubt it was
that Inca lout."
"It was the gun," somebody roared, "that shot and killed him
from the floor."
The gun exploded from the floor: it's in the script and in the
score.

Before he died, the noble sire cursed Leonore with smoldering
ire.
"My curse's on your head," he said, gave up the ghost and then
expired.
Leonore with the Inca flee. Both get lost in this potpourri.
They never meet again, you'll see, until the last act agony.

ACT II

Scene 1. The Kitchen of the Inn in Hornacuelos.

This scene is full of noise and cheer, peasants and smelly
muleteers;
And sure enough Don Carlo's there, seeking the killer, debonair.
Carlito wasn't home the night his dad was killed and Sis took
flight;
But ever since that fatal night, he's sworn he'll kill the two on
sight.

Coincidence, as you will see, again starts working mysterics.
Leonore, too, comes to the inn; imagine, runs right into him!
Although they both meet vis-à-vis, he does not recognize it's she.
She's dressed in men's clothes—bourgeoisie—to hide her own
identity.

More oft than not, in men's attire, a prima donna's not so hot,
Especially the dramatic ones, with double breasts and you know
what!

151

Leonore prays that she'll escape unseen her brother and his
wrath.
She weeps and cries and wants to die, but not be killed by that
psychopath.

Here Preziosilla crashes in, recruiting men for war and things.
She praises war, tells fortunes, too, still acting like a ding-a-ling.
She beats the drum, gets bold and tough, and does more "join
the Army" stuff.
With any luck, this scene is cut—often, but not often enough.

And now some pressure's brought to bear; the phony student
must declare
Just who he is and where he's from, his calling and his *nom de
guerre.*
He tells the Mayor he's on the scent of an assassin and hell-bent
To find the murderer who killed the father of his dearest friend.

It's his own story; then he says that since he cannot help his
friend,
To Salamanca he'll return for his degree, and that's the end.
"Hasta la vista," they all beam, prepared to leave the old canteen.
The curtain falls on this routine and ends this somewhat mess
in scene.

Scene 2. At the Convent Gate at Hornacuelos.

"At last I'm here," said Leonore, just as she reached the convent
gate;
In trembling fear she pulls the cord that rings the bell above the
grate.
She dries the tears from both her eyes, then sadly sighs with
trembling lips,
"What a narrow escape I had, to give the murderer the slip."

Fra Melitone fumed, wheezed and foamed, a lantern in his hand.
"Who's there," he groaned, "this time of night, roaming this
sacred land?"

152

"I know it's late, but I can't wait. I must see your superior."
"That's easier said than done," said he, "but I'll inform
    El Superior."

The old monk thought it was a man, because of the person's
    attire,
And as he stumbled on, he said, "I hope I'll find the Holy Prior;
But if I don't come back at once, don't stick around, you hear?"
Then, murmuring to himself he said, "Well, sure enough, that
    guy looks queer."

In fright and fear she hears the sound of old feet scraping on the
    ground.
Father Guardiano then appears and asks in basso tones profound,
"Who are you, sir? What seek you here? Speak up, don't be
    afraid."
He learns it is the Vargas girl, dressed as a man in masquerade.

In deep distress, she tells the rest, her father's curse, her fright
    and fear.
The old monk listens, more or less, and even tries to shed a tear.
She'll give up life, the world, the flesh, if the good Father will
    consent
To let her stay, sing hymns and pray, and be a devout penitent.

"You've sure got spunk," said the good monk, "so you may stick
    around.
We've got a cave, once occupied, within these holy, sacred
    grounds.
In a monk's robe, mid rocks and coves, you can pray there both
    day and night.
I'll send a loaf of bread at times, and water, too. Bless you; sit
    tight."

Then all the monks march out in file, a glowing candle in each
    hand.
"May any soul drop dead on sight, who dares to cross this holy
    land."

153

And more, the Holy Father says, "Let Heaven any prowler
  smote.
May he be stricken utterly; his ashes scattered"—end of quote.

He then says, "Rise, be on your way. No living soul more shall
  you see.
The cave bell will give warning, should danger threaten thee;
And just in case you should drop dead, your soul we'll comfort
  as it flees."
Then one and all the good monks left, leaving her to her destiny.

ACT III

A Military Camp Somewhere in Italy

And talk about coincidence, the stars, and fate, and destiny,
Alvaro and Don Carlo are in the same camp in Italy.
How both got there incognito is neither here nor there;
In opera, as in love and war, absurdity is more than fair.

Alvaro goes on quite a bit about his birth and pedigree.
He's noble on his father's side, who, too, was a Spanish grandee.
He tried in vain away from Spain a kingdom to create,
Married an Inca, made a flop, was thrown in jail—ah, cruel Fate!

He also thinks his Leonore has gone to Heaven long ago,
And that she's now among the saints, pure and white as snow.
"Oh, help me, divine spirit," he pleads to her he thinks on high.
"Have mercy on my suffering, and pray I soon may die."

Another bit of happenstance, believe it if you will or can,
Carlo gets mixed up in a brawl with cutthroats from a robber
  gang.
He screams for help as he's attacked, about to lose his life,
Cheated at cards, by scum at large, with *navajas* and knives.

He's saved just in the nick of time from murderers that flee.
Alvaro brings him back alive. For crying out loud—that's destiny!

"How can a guy of noble birth, a fact that's plain to see,
Get mixed up with those lousy hoods?" Alvaro says. "Enlighten
me."

They both tell lies and try to hide their true identity;
Give *noms de guerre*, then vow and swear eternal fealty.
Then hand in hand the *bonne camarades* rush off to win the war;
Fight side by side, with Spanish pride, like latter-day
conquistadors.

The Three Wise Fates, cold and ingrate, that spin, stretch
thread and snip,
Are never late to keep a date and start out gaily on this trip.
A battlefield's grist to their mill, so as they laugh, frolic and
chide,
They've jotted down Alvaro's name; perhaps they'll take him
for a ride.

Alvaro's wounded in the chest, fighting in war in Italy.
Both he and Carlo, side by side, it's fate or else astrology.
Alvaro prays that he will die; he's had it, so hopes it's the end.
Don Carlo gives him loving care—a friend in need indeed's a
friend.

"You'll win the Calatrava prize because of your brave deeds."
So says Don Carlo to his friend, who loathes that very name and
breed.
"Of Calatrava, never!" cries Don Alvaro breathlessly,
Which makes Don Carlo stop to think, could this be force of
destiny?

Alvaro hands Carlo a case, before they start the great duet
Of pledges, word-of-honor vows, mid blood and tears and sweat.
The great Hidalgo swears and vows by all that's holy, he'll be
true.
If Al should die, he'll burn the case. Alvaro says, *"Merci
beaucoup."*

Now he can die in peace and grace. He thanks his friend time
 and again.
His secret will be burned, thank God; he's sure, alas, this is
 his end.
Don Carlo has a qualm or two, besides Alvaro still alive;
But could it be that it is he, the guy that ruined his family life?

"How sad to die," he starts to cry, "death is indeed an awful
 thing;
But I can't buy that alibi, all about 'Death, where is thy
 sting?' "
Then as he thinks, still stranger things keep popping
 in his mind;
Bound on revenge, he won't give up, until the day his prey he'll
 find.

So, like the great aristocrat, he still believes in tit for tat.
Not to defend one's honor's like—the same as straining at a gnat.
And though his conscience bothers him, he's planning to untie
 the string;
Besides, he'll only take a peek; then burn the case and all the
 things.

He has another qualm or two, then he breaks through Alvaro's
 case.
A portrait falls upon the ground—"*Mio Dios*," it's Leonore's
 face.
"It's he," he screams, "that S.O.B.; at last I've got that rat.
I'll murder him, that's what I'll do," so spake the great
 aristocrat.

Just then the surgeon of the camp says joyfully, "Your friend
 will live."
"But not for long, I'll swear to that, that half-breed Inca
 fugitive."
Alvaro rushes through the door, starts to embrace the grand
 señor.

"I'm well again, my faithful friend, and even stronger than
   before."

"Cut out that false camaraderie; prepare to meet your destiny."
"I don't quite understand," says Al. "Are you perhaps joking
   with me?"
"You'll pay for your vile felony," Don Carlo says. "Soon you
   will see."
"Oh, now I see it clear," says Al. "You broke your sacred vow,
   Grandee."

"So what," says Carlo, mad as hell, "and that goes for that
   Jezebel;
My sister, who else would I mean; she made the Calatrava
   name unclean."
"She lives," cries Al. "That lamb of God, you tell me that she's
   living still?
I'll find and wed her on the spot." Don Carlo says, "Like hell
   you will."

Then just in time, before a crime, the ragged soldiers march
   across.
They stop the two belligerents who once again stray and get lost.
And Preziosilla's back again, with her Salvation Army stuff.
The curtain falls and just in time. Enough is quite more than
   enough.

ACT IV

Scene 1. The Courtyard of the Church of the Angels

This strange plot thickens more and more, although five years
   have passed.
Don Carlo, still bent on revenge, has sought and found his prey
   at last.
Coincidence and mystery, with much more force of destiny,
Have brought together, as you'll see, the more or less unholy
   three.

157

Alvaro, now Fra Rafael, has donned the cloth, his soul to quell.
Leonore's practically next door, mid rocks and crags in her dim
cell.
Don Carlo, still on vengeance bound, has found the holy, pious
place.
He swears this time Alvaro'll die; he'll pay the price for his
disgrace.

Within the holy citadel, he asks to see Fra Rafael.
Alvaro greets Carlo with joy, much more than even tongue can
tell.
"Just knock off all that camaraderie, and all that phony 'glad
to see.'
This time you'll die, or maybe me. It all depends on destiny."

"Son of a bitch," the friar yells. This time Alvaro's mad as hell.
" 'Tis you who desecrates these grounds, you Torquemada
infidel."
Don Carlo carries, to make sure, two swords and other
armament.
This time they'll fight unto the end; then Fra Rafael starts to
repent.

"Have mercy on a penitent," then drops the sword upon the
ground.
"Let not Hell triumph, go in peace," then bows his head in
prayer profound.
"You flout me, coward, mulatto base," then slaps the friar in
the face.
"You've sealed your fate," says Fra Rafael, "let it be death."—
Away they race.

Scene 2. A Valley amid Rocks; a Stream; also a Cave

The Three Wise Fates and Destiny pursue Leonore relentlessly.
She prays for peace and harmony, there where now all is serenity.
She moans her fate, alas too late, as she berates cruel destiny.
She can't forget Alvaro, yet she knows what is to be will be.

158

She takes a breath, then prays for death and hopes it will come
soon.
We hear the sound of clashing swords as the belligerents near
their doom.
Leonore rushes to her cave, with sobs and tears, and moans and
sighs.
She shuts the door, sad and heart-sore, and then she starts to
vocalize.

Again a dying voice is heard, "Rush for a priest, my soul to
save.
I must be shriven 'fore I die." Alvaro rushes to the cave.
"Please, Mr. Hermit, please, I beg. A man who's dying must
confess."
"I cannot come, can't tell you why; I'm not allowed to shrive or
bless."

"A woman's voice. Ah, no, a ghost! I'm going mad. It cannot be."
Santa Maria, it is Leonore. He starts to swoon and says, "It's
she."
Wounded and more dead than alive, supported by some dear
old monks,
Before he dies, Carlo revives, and stabs Leonore to death, the
skunk.

"How odd of God," Alvaro sobs, "to wreak this vengeance on
Leonore."
"Please hold your tongue," a friar says. "How dare you question
El Señor?"
Mid psalms and tears, praises and prayers, "Gloria in Excelsis"
everywhere,
Leonore dies, amid good-byes, and vows to met her love Up
There!

"Oh, please don't leave me, Leonore. Heaven can wait. Please,
I implore."
"Alas, I must. Heaven is just, and I'll be waiting on that shore."

Some scripts say Al jumped from a cliff, and some just leave him
  then and there.
What Destiny has up its sleeve, we'll never know, and, well,
  who cares?

And now that you've read who did what to whom, and all that
  tommyrot,
You'll be bewildered and confused, perplexed and dazed—at
  least somewhat.
There's no such thing as an impossible dream, believe in this
  or not;
But you'll confess and acquiesce, there is such a thing as an
  impossible plot.